SO-ANE-348

Yesterday, Today, & Forever

Yesterday, Today, & Forever

KATHI MILLS

HERALD PRESS
Scottdale, Pennsylvania
Kitchener, Ontario

Library of Congress Cataloging-in-Publication Data

Mills, Kathi, 1948-
   Yesterday, today, and forever / Kathi Mills.
     p. cm.
   ISBN 0-8361-3488-5
   I. Title.
PS3563.I42319Y47   1989   88-27266
813'.54—dc19   CIP

The paper used in this publication meets the minimum requirements of American National Standard for Information Sciences—Permanence of Paper for Printed Library Materials, ANSI Z39.48-1984.

YESTERDAY, TODAY, AND FOREVER

Copyright © 1989 by Herald Press, Scottdale, Pa. 15683
   Published simultaneously in Canada by Herald Press,
   Kitchener, Ont. N2G 4M5. All rights reserved.
Library of Congress Catalog Card Number: 88-27266
International Standard Book Number: 0-8361-3488-5
Printed in the United States of America
Cover art by Susan K. Hunsberger
Book design by Paula M. Johnson

95 94 93 92 91 90 89 10 9 8 7 6 5 4 3 2 1

To Larry
My strongest supporter
My greatest encourager
My kindest critic

Chapter 1

Rachel paced catlike across the length of the expansive living room. She stopped in front of the picture window, peering anxiously into the darkness in a vain attempt to glimpse approaching headlights on the long, circular driveway.

Where is he? she fumed for the hundredth time that evening. She chewed a nail nervously, then stopped, self-consciously jamming her fists into the pockets of her loose-fitting kimono. Bill hates it when I bite my nails. She sighed, then pulled her hands back out of her pockets and defiantly chewed another nail. Who cares what he likes or doesn't like? she thought, turning and plopping down on the stiff white love seat.

"I hate this chair!" she grumbled, reaching for a piece of candy from the crystal serving dish on the coffee table. Popping the candy into her mouth, she glanced around the room. The sparkling chrome and glass furnishings seemed to mock her. Not only do I hate this chair, she thought, snatching up another piece of candy, I hate this house.

She closed her eyes, savoring the sweet caramel taste as she chewed, and thought of how it had been before they moved to this house fifteen years earlier. Rachel had loved the little duplex where they had lived when she and Bill were first married, and where they had brought their only child, Jennifer, home from the hospital when she was born three years after their marriage. It was a small home, furnished mostly with antiques, which had belonged to Rachel's grandparents. Rachel had always felt comfortable there—and safe. The small fenced yard had been so easy to care for, and so perfect for Jennifer to play in.

Rachel had spent many sunny afternoons working in her garden while Jennifer played under her mother's watchful eye.

And then Bill's general contracting company had begun to grow. Rachel had naively hoped that, once the business got off the ground, Bill would be free to spend more time with her and Jennifer. It had proved to be just the opposite.

Rachel had resented the increasing number of hours Bill devoted to the business; she also deeply resented their move. Bill had insisted they needed a larger home for entertaining once the company was doing well, but Rachel had never felt she belonged in the sprawling, two-story house. And when Bill had relegated her grandparents' antiques to the attic in favor of the new modern furniture, she had been furious.

But, after all her arguing and crying, in the end she had given in. They had moved to the new house when Jennifer was seven years old, had bought the furnishings that Rachel considered cold and sterile, and had even hired a man to come in twice a week and take care of the huge yard and swimming pool. The one thing Rachel had refused to budge on, however, was the idea of getting a housekeeper. Bill argued that the house was too big for Rachel to keep up by herself, but she was adamant about not having someone else doing her job for her.

Rachel jumped when she felt Snuffy's cold wet nose rubbing against her arm. She opened her eyes and looked affectionately into the warm brown eyes of their family collie. Snuffy had been around for more than fourteen years now. Bill had brought him home one evening as a surprise for Jennifer soon after they had moved into the new house.

It had been love at first sight for Jennifer and Snuffy (so christened by Jennifer because he spent so much time sniffing out his new surroundings). But Rachel had been appalled. She had always been terrified of dogs. Bill knew that, and she was hurt by what she considered his lack of sensitivity. At first, she had refused to have anything to do with Snuffy, but the puppy seemed to sense the problem and set out to remedy it. He followed Rachel around during the day, nuzzling her any time she stood still long enough for him to get a chance. It wasn't long before his soulful eyes and cute puppy ways had won her heart. Now she wondered how she had ever gotten along without him.

She hugged him, stroking his long silky fur. "You're such a good dog," she crooned, as he wagged his tail happily. "At least I can always count on you, can't I, Snuf?"

Snuffy barked in agreement.

Which is more than I can say for some people, she thought, checking her watch. It was almost ten. "Okay, that does it!" she exclaimed, reaching for the phone on the end table beside her. "I know he doesn't like me to call him at work when he's late, but this is ridiculous."

She let the phone ring fifteen times before slamming it back into its cradle. Tears of frustration burned her eyelids as she jumped up and hurried into the kitchen to check on what was left of dinner.

"Great!" she muttered, opening the oven door. "Just great. This is the third meal I've ruined this month waiting for him to come home."

Rachel sat down at the table and grabbed a dinner roll from the basket, buttering it liberally. She wasn't really hungry but, somehow, chewing the roll made her feel better. She was about to bite into a second roll when she heard a key in the front door.

"Well, it's about time!" She jumped up and stormed out to meet her husband.

Bill was standing in the entryway with his suit jacket draped over one arm, his tie hanging loosely across his shoulder, his shirt rumpled and sweat-stained. Beads of perspiration stood out on his forehead and he needed a shave, but, even in her anger, Rachel was aware of what an attractive man her husband was.

Bill reached down to pet Snuffy, scarcely looking at Rachel. "Whew, it's hot! Those blasted Santa Ana winds—they're the curse of southern California." He shook his head wearily. "Man, am I glad it's Friday."

As he walked toward her, he glanced at the dinner roll in Rachel's hand. "I thought you were on a diet. What are you doing eating rolls so late in the evening? You know you're not supposed to eat anything after dinner. You're never going to lose that twenty pounds at this rate."

Rachel could feel her face growing hot. She tried to keep her voice calm. "This," she began through clenched teeth, holding up the roll, "is not an after-dinner snack. For your information, I have not yet had dinner. I've been waiting for you."

"Oh, for Pete's sake, Rachel," Bill answered disgustedly, "didn't you get my message?"

Rachel, still holding the roll in front of her, was suddenly flustered. "What message? I didn't get any message."

Bill brushed past her angrily and strode to the answering machine beside the phone in the kitchen. Rachel came in behind him in time to hear the tape informing her, "Hi, it's me. I'll be late tonight, so don't hold dinner."

"That message!" Bill answered sarcastically, flicking off the machine and turning to stare at her. "The message on the phone recorder—the recorder I bought so we wouldn't miss any important messages, remember? You know, the one you always forget to check. Damn, Rachel—"

"Don't you curse at me, Bill Webster!" she warned, her dark eyes flashing. "And don't try to turn this around so that I'm at fault. You're the one who's never home. Never! And I'm sick of it, do you hear? The only time I see you is when we have to go to one of your stupid dinner meetings."

"Stupid!" Bill threw his jacket down on the kitchen table, knocking over the vase of flowers that Rachel had arranged earlier that day. The vase rolled off the table and crashed onto the floor, shattering instantly, as the sweet smell of roses mingled with the aroma of overdone roast. Neither Rachel nor Bill seemed to notice. Snuffy, who had followed them into the kitchen, cowered under the table.

"So, you think my meetings are stupid, do you? I suppose you think my friends are stupid, too! And what about my business? Is that stupid? You sure don't seem to mind spending any of my money that I make on my stupid business, do you?"

Rachel squeezed the dinner roll until it crumbled between her fingers. She spoke slowly and deliberately. "Your money? Your business? Well, at least you're finally being honest. You always have considered it your business and your money, haven't you? And your house and your cars and your—"

"That's enough, Rachel!"

"No!" Rachel went on, her voice rising now. "No, Bill, it's not enough. None of this is enough. Because if it's all yours, what's in it for me? I don't even have a husband anymore. You never have any time for me. You're always down at your precious business working—or whatever."

Bill's face changed. The anger was gone, but Rachel couldn't tell what it was that had taken its place. His voice became guarded. "What's that supposed to mean, Rachel?"

Suddenly, Rachel's anger was gone, too. "Never mind," she mumbled. "Forget it."

"No, Rachel," Bill insisted. "I want to know what you meant by 'whatever.'"

"I didn't mean anything," Rachel answered nervously, turning to walk away.

Bill grabbed her arm. "Don't walk away from me, Rachel. We've started this thing—let's finish it."

Rachel looked down at Bill's hand on her arm, then back up into his eyes. "Let go of my arm," she ordered coolly.

Bill dropped his hand. "I'm sorry. But I want you to stay here and talk to me."

"I have nothing more to say to you," Rachel answered, lowering her gaze and walking quickly into the living room.

Bill was right behind her. "Well, maybe I have something to say to you."

She turned to face him, a twitch beginning over her right eye. "I'm tired, Bill," she said flatly. "I'd like to go to bed now."

"Later," Bill answered. "We're going to talk first. It's a talk we should have had years ago. We're not going to put it off any longer."

They stared at each other in silence for a moment, then Rachel walked over to the love seat and sank down resignedly. Bill sat down next to her. Rachel's palms were clammy, and the twitch over her eye was growing worse. She waited for Bill to speak.

He took a deep breath. "Rachel, there are so many things I want to say to you—things I've needed to say for so long. Somehow it just never seemed to be the right time or place."

Rachel stared at her hands as she twisted her wedding ring nervously. She couldn't bring herself to look up.

Bill cleared his throat. "Rachel, I know I haven't been a very good husband lately—in fact, for a long time now. I'm not sure when it happened—I'm not even sure what happened—but I do know things are not the way we hoped they would be when we first got married." He paused, his voice almost a whisper. "I loved you so much then, Rachel."

A faint ringing had begun in Rachel's ears, and she was having a difficult time concentrating on Bill's words. She felt as if she were floating high above the room, watching but not participating in the conversation. "I don't want to talk about this, Bill."

"We have to, Rachel." Bill's voice was quiet now, gentle. Rachel wished he were still yelling at her.

Bill tried to take her hand, but she stiffened, and he let go. "Rachel, listen to me, please. You know I never wanted things to turn out like this. We had so many dreams when we got married, so many plans. Do you remember how we used to sit out on our porch back at the other house in the evenings and talk about how things would be when we got older? The trips we'd take, the things we'd see and do."

Rachel tried in vain to will her eye to stop twitching. "Maybe it's not too late to do those things now," she whispered, still not daring to look up.

Bill stared at his wife for a moment, then stood and began pacing in short, quick turns. Rachel sat very still, scarcely breathing. She wondered why she felt smothered. Maybe the air conditioner had stopped working.

"Rachel." Bill's voice made her jump. She forced herself to look at him. He stood in front of her, running his fingers anxiously through his thick dark hair. Their eyes met and he knelt down in front of her, taking both her hands firmly in his. This time she didn't pull away.

The tears in his eyes broke her heart. She wanted to put her arms around him, to hold him close, but she sat very still.

"Rachel," he began, "I'm so sorry. I never meant to hurt you. You know that, don't you? I always wanted the best for you. I wanted to give you everything. And for years, I thought that's what I was doing. By the time I realized I was wrong, it was too late. You had changed somehow. You weren't the same woman I'd married. I didn't know what to say to you, how to reach you."

He blinked, and a tear rolled slowly down his cheek. "I tried," he went on. "I did, Rachel. Really! But, somewhere along the line, I just gave up." He sighed and shrugged helplessly. "I don't know. You seemed so wrapped up in taking care of Jennifer and this house, your church work, the charities. We each seemed to have found our own lives, I suppose. So I told myself that was okay. You'd lead your life, I'd lead mine. But it just hasn't worked out, Rachel. It just hasn't worked out."

Rachel groped desperately for something positive to say, something to prove to him that he was wrong, that things could be good for them again. "I could change," she offered, so quietly she wasn't sure if she'd said it aloud or just thought it. "I could be a better wife."

Bill squeezed her hands. "No!" He shook his head. "You just don't understand, do you? Rachel, it's too late! Can't you see that? I'm not asking you to change. You've always been a good wife. You're a wonderful cook and housekeeper, a perfect mother—that's just not the point any longer!"

"Then what is?" she cried, finding her voice at last. "What is it you want from me, Bill?"

"I want my freedom, Rachel," he answered slowly. "I want a divorce."

Rachel couldn't have been more horrified if he'd slapped her. She stared at him, wide-eyed. Those brown eyes she had once thought so tender and gentle now terrified her. Who was this man? When had he come to live in her husband's body? Why was he trying to hurt her? Suddenly, she was aware of his hands holding hers. She snatched them away as if they were on fire, clamping them over her mouth.

Bill stood up, shifting from one foot to the other. "Well. . . ." He brushed the wetness from his eyes. "If you don't feel like talking anymore right now, I think it would be best if I just went upstairs and packed some things. I'll get a room somewhere tonight, and then I'll come back for the rest of my stuff later. We'll talk some more whenever you're ready."

He hesitated, but when she didn't answer, he turned and walked toward the hallway. Halfway up the stairs he stopped, gripping the smooth wooden banister until his knuckles turned white. Then he went on up to their bedroom and started pulling suits and shirts from the closet.

As he was laying them out on their king-sized bed, the door burst open. "Just what do you think you're doing?" Rachel demanded, her face red and her eyes blazing as she moved toward him.

Bill frowned. "I told you, Rachel. I'm packing. I'm going to a motel and—"

Rachel snatched up his clothes from the bed and threw them in crumpled piles on the floor. "You're not going anywhere!" she screamed. "I'm your wife. You can't leave me. You can't!" She began hitting him in the chest with her fists. "I won't let you. I won't let you leave me."

Bill stood there, silent and unmoving, until she collapsed onto the floor in tears. Then he lifted her gently and helped her onto the bed. "Shhh," he whispered. "It's all right, Rachel. It's all right. Everything's going to be all right. Just lie down here and rest." He sat beside her and stroked her hair until she was quiet. Her eyes closed and her breathing became slow and steady.

"Can you sleep for a while now, Rachel?"

She didn't answer.

Bill rose carefully and pulled a comforter over her. Turning out the light, he tiptoed out of the bedroom, closing the door behind him. Once downstairs, he poured himself a drink, then went into the kitchen where Snuffy greeted him warily.

"It's okay, Snuf," Bill reassured him with a pat. "Everything is okay, boy."

He picked up the phone and dialed, holding his ice-cold drink against his throbbing temple. Sheryl answered on the first ring.

"Hello?"

"Sheryl."

"Oh, darling! I thought you'd never call! Is everything okay? Did you talk to her? Are you coming over?"

"Everything's fine, honey. Don't worry. Yes, we talked."

"About us? What did she say?"

Bill hesitated. "Well, we didn't actually talk about us . . . ."

"But, Bill, you said you were going home to tell her about us. You promised."

"I know I promised," Bill answered, "but I never got the chance. She was so angry when I got home that we got into a big fight. But, sweetheart, I did tell her I wanted a divorce. I just didn't tell her about you or the baby yet. Maybe it's just as well. She's pretty upset."

"Where is she?"

"Sleeping. Which, by the way, you should be, too. You have to take care of yourself now that you're pregnant, you know."

"Does that mean you're not coming over? Oh, Bill, you said you'd be here tonight."

"I know, honey. I know. And believe me, I want to! In fact, I was packing, but she got so hysterical. I just couldn't leave her like that, Sheryl. Not until morning. Then I'll call Jennifer to come and stay with her. I promise."

Sheryl sighed. "All right. I suppose I can live without you for one more night. But that's it, Bill Webster! Do you hear me?"

Bill smiled. "I hear you, Sheryl Matthews. And I love you. Good night."

Bill hung up the phone and turned to see Rachel standing in the kitchen doorway.

Chapter 2

Bill's mouth fell open and his drink shook in his hand as he stared at his wife. Neither of them spoke. Bill took a step toward Rachel, his arms outstretched as if in a peace offering.

"Don't you come near me," Rachel ordered. "Don't you ever come near me again!"

"Rachel, please, let me explain."

"There's nothing left to explain. I understand everything now. And I don't care to hear any of the sordid details. Just pack your things and get out."

"But, Rachel, I don't want to leave you alone like this."

"You left me alone a long time ago, Bill Webster. Now, get your things and go! Sheryl and . . . your baby . . . need you."

Bill's eyes filled with tears. "I didn't mean for you to find out this way."

"Obviously."

"Rachel, maybe we should talk."

Rachel's eyes were cold and hard. "I have nothing more to say to you, Bill."

Bill stared at his wife helplessly, then walked slowly, carefully past her and up the stairs to finish packing.

Rachel looked at the table with its unused dishes and silverware, the linen napkins still rolled snugly in their rings. They seemed out of place sitting there next to Bill's rumpled jacket, which had landed on top of the bread basket. The water stains from the spilled vase had already dried on the tablecloth, but Rachel could see the outlines where they had been. She was suddenly overwhelmed with an urge to sit down and cry. Instead, she cleared the table, then brought a broom and dustpan to clean up the broken vase. As she dumped the pieces of the vase into the trash, she stared at them, feeling herself being sucked into a deep, dark hole, as tears once again threatened her.

"No!" She shook her head. "I am not going to cry."

She threw the burned roast in on top of the broken vase, then noticed the answering machine next to the phone. Bill's sarcasm echoed in her ears, as she fumbled with the wires, unhooking the answering machine from the phone and tossing it into the trash, along with the roast and the broken vase. She loaded the dishwasher and turned it on, then looked around at her spotless kitchen. Everything was back in order once again.

Rachel heard the front door close, and she knew he was gone.

* * *

"Mom? Mom, where are you?"

Rachel sat up with a start. What's happening? What's wrong? She looked around, trying to focus. Why was she in the kitchen?

Snuffy jumped up from where he had been sleeping at Rachel's feet and barked excitedly. He was staring at something, his tail wagging furiously. Rachel followed his gaze to the kitchen door—and then she remembered. Bill. Sheryl. A baby.

She looked at her watch. Six-thirty. Had she slept with her head on the kitchen table all night?

"Mom, are you in here?" Jennifer hurried through the kitchen door, her face taut and strained. She ignored Snuffy as he greeted her, jumping and whining for her attention. "Oh, Mom. Are you all right?"

Rachel stood up stiffly, her muscles sore and aching, and put her arms around her daughter. "Oh, Mama!" Jennifer cried. "I came as soon as Daddy called me. I can't believe any of this." She stood back and looked at Rachel, as tears trickled slowly down her cheeks. "Is it true, Mom? You and Dad are getting a divorce?"

The pain on Jennifer's face broke Rachel's heart. How she

wanted to be able to assure her that everything was all right, the way she used to when Jennifer was little and woke up during the night from a bad dream. But this time it was more than just a bad dream, and Rachel knew there was nothing she could say or do to make things better again.

She reached up and put her hand on Jennifer's soft young face, marveling at her daughter's natural beauty. She had Rachel's dark violet eyes, and Bill's thick black curly hair. No matter how Jennifer tried to tame her hair or pull it back off her face, there always seemed to be one or two unruly locks that escaped and curled defiantly around her forehead or cheeks. All the years Jennifer was growing up, she had complained about her curls, wanting to wear her hair long and straight the way her girlfriends did. Rachel, with her straight brown hair pulled back in a severe bun, would look at her beautiful daughter and think how glad she was that, other than her eyes, Jennifer looked like her father. Now, realizing how much Jennifer truly did look like Bill, Rachel winced in pain.

"I'm so sorry, darling," Rachel whispered. She took Jennifer's hands and held them tightly. "Let's go into the other room and sit down."

Jennifer nodded, and they walked slowly, arms around each other for support, toward the living room. Snuffy followed them, his head tilted curiously to one side.

Suddenly, the memory of Bill, kneeling in front of her, asking her for a divorce, flashed through Rachel's mind. "No." She stopped. "Not in the living room. Let's go into the den where it's more comfortable."

"Sure, Mom."

As they sat down on the cool beige leather-covered couch in front of the fireplace, Rachel wondered how she could possibly explain any of this to Jennifer. How much had Bill told her? How much did she really need to know? She looked so much younger and more innocent than her twenty-two years, sitting there in her pink sundress, her long hair pulled back off her face in a matching pink ribbon. The few curls that had worked their way loose from the ribbon only made her look sweeter—more vulnerable, Rachel thought.

She sighed. She had missed Jennifer desperately since she had married Chuck Miller six months earlier and moved up the coast thirty miles to Santa Barbara. Rachel liked her son-in-law very much, and they all visited back and forth regularly, but she hadn't quite adjusted to the fact that her only child was now a married woman with a life of her own.

"Mama?" Jennifer's eyes were pleading with her mother. "Mama, what are we going to do?"

Rachel shook her head. "I don't know, Jenny. I really don't know." She took a deep breath and tried to smile. "We'll do what we have to do, I suppose. We'll go on, one day at a time, as we always have. There's no other choice, is there, dear?"

"But, Mother, why? Why does Dad want a divorce? I know it's Dad that wants it, and not you. I know that. But why now? What's happened between you two? Is there someone else?"

Rachel tried to maintain her composure, but the flicker of pain on her face was obvious.

"That's it, isn't it?" Jennifer gasped. "Dad wants a divorce because he's in love with someone else. Oh, God!" She buried her face in her hands and sobbed, rocking back and forth, as Rachel stroked her hair and tried to calm her. As her sobs lessened, Jennifer looked up at her mother, her eyes red and swollen. "How could he do this, Mom? I don't understand. How could he?"

Rachel closed her eyes briefly and sighed. "I don't know, honey. I don't know." She looked down at her hands, folded now in her lap. "These things just happen, I suppose. You hear about it all the time."

"Well, they don't happen in our family!" Jennifer cried. "I think it's disgusting. And I intend to tell him so. Where is he?"

"It doesn't matter where he is, Jenny. He's made his choice. Now we all have to live with it."

"Why?" Jennifer demanded. "Why do we have to live with it? I certainly don't have to. And you shouldn't, either." Jennifer looked at her mother earnestly. "Mom, it won't last, I know it. Daddy will realize what he's done and come back. I'm sure of it. Whoever she is, I know he doesn't really love her. He couldn't. It's just some cheap affair, and Daddy will see that and come home."

Rachel squared her shoulders and looked at her daughter. "There's one thing you must understand, Jennifer. Your father has left me for another woman. Whether that works out or not, I will not have him back here with me. There will be no forgiveness, no second chances. I don't want him back—not now, not ever!"

Jennifer frowned. "Oh, Mama, I know you're saying that because you're hurt, but someday you'll feel differently."

"No, Jennifer," Rachel answered firmly. "There will be no someday for your father and me. It's over. You may as well accept that."

"But, Mama, you could fight for him."

"Fight for him!" Rachel exploded. "Fight for him? And just what would you suggest I do? Put on a sexy negligee and go parading over to his little love nest and ring the doorbell? Sheryl's twenty years younger than I am, and even in her pregnant condition, probably looks twice as good as I could ever hope to look again. Fight for him! I wouldn't humiliate myself."

Rachel suddenly realized what she had said. She stopped and looked at her daughter. Jennifer's face, beet-red only a few minutes earlier, had changed to a deathly white.

"Oh, Jenny," Rachel whispered, horrified. "Jenny, I'm sorry. I wasn't going to tell you any of that." She tried to put her arms around her daughter, but Jennifer stiffened and stared at Rachel.

"Sheryl? Sheryl Matthews? Dad is having an affair with his secretary? I can't believe it. It's like some horrible soap opera or something." She shook her head, then looked at Rachel again, wide-eyed. "And she's pregnant?"

Before Rachel could answer, she heard Snuffy barking and realized the doorbell was ringing. She looked at her watch. "It's not even seven yet. Who in the world could be ringing the doorbell at this hour of the morning?"

"Maybe it's Dad," Jennifer offered, as they walked into the entryway.

Rachel shook her head. "I doubt it. Besides, he still has his key. He would have let himself in, just the way you did." She looked through the peephole, then turned to Jennifer. "It's Aunt Mavis!" she announced, stunned. "What in the world?"

"Oh, no! I forgot. I called her before I came over," Jennifer explained. "I told her that Dad had called and what he said, and asked her to come over if she hadn't heard from me in a while. I'm sorry, Mom. I was just so worried."

"Great," Rachel sighed, reaching for the doorknob. "Just what I need right now—Aunt Mavis!"

* * *

Aunt Mavis bustled in as she always did—mouth first. "Oh, my dears," she began, seeing Rachel and Jennifer standing together, "I'm so relieved to see you're both all right. I can't tell you how worried I was when Jenny called. It's so confusing, all this talk about Bill leaving." She interrupted herself to pat her short gray hair into place, then went on. "Well, now that I'm here, let's sit down and talk about this nonsense, shall we?"

With her purse still slung over one arm, she grabbed Rachel and Jennifer and steered them past Snuffy into the living room. Pointing them toward the love seat, she plopped down across from them in a low-slung recliner, nearly tipping it over. "Oh, my!" she exclaimed. "I'd forgotten how uncomfortable this chair is."

"Would you like to move into another room, Aunt Mavis?" Rachel asked hopefully, as Snuffy lay down at her feet.

"Oh, no, my dear," Aunt Mavis answered, rearranging herself, "this will do just fine. Now, where were we?"

Rachel and Jennifer looked at each other, and then at Aunt Mavis. Rachel cleared her throat. "Well . . . ."

"Of course!" Aunt Mavis interrupted, "I remember. We were

going to discuss this business about Bill." She looked at Jennifer. "Did I understand you correctly? Did you tell me that Bill left? Left for where? Is this a permanent situation?"

Jennifer blushed. She opened her mouth as if to speak, but it was Rachel who answered.

"Yes, Aunt Mavis," she explained as steadily as she possibly could. "Yes, it's a permanent situation, I'm afraid. Bill and I are getting a divorce."

"Well!" Aunt Mavis exclaimed, clucking her tongue. "Well, well! This will never do." Suddenly she blinked and looked back at Jennifer. "And just where is your husband? He's not gone, too, I hope!"

Jennifer's eyes opened wide. "Aunt Mavis, of course not! Chuck's coming down as soon as he clears up some morning appointments. He wanted to come with me, but I convinced him to take care of things at the office first." She glanced at her watch. "I'm sure he'll be here by noon."

"Good," Aunt Mavis nodded, apparently satisfied that all was well with Jennifer and Chuck. "That's good. It's important for a pastor to keep his appointments." She smiled. "Especially when it's his first pastorate. Such a nice young man, your Chuck. I always did like him."

Jennifer smiled weakly. "Thank you, Aunt Mavis."

"What do you suppose has gotten into him?" Aunt Mavis asked, turning back to Rachel.

It took Rachel a moment to realize Aunt Mavis was talking about Bill again. Before she could respond, Aunt Mavis went on. "Of course, these things seldom happen suddenly. Obviously, it's been building up for some time. I've suspected there was a problem between the two of you for several years now, but I never could quite put my finger on it. I mean, neither of you ever said anything, but something's been eating at your marriage for a long time, like a horde of unseen termites! If you don't nip these things in the bud, you know, they just grow and grow until it's too late!" She clucked her tongue again and sighed. "Well, of course, you know there's only one thing for us to do."

Rachel was too shocked to ask just what that one thing might be. Besides, she knew very well that Aunt Mavis was going to tell her, whether she wanted to know or not.

"We're going to pray for him," Aunt Mavis announced with a satisfied grin. "Oh, I know what you're thinking. We've been praying for him for years, but sometimes it takes something like this to bring people around." She looked at Rachel. "You know, my dear, I was so concerned when you married Bill. You were so young—and so in love. Do you remember how your parents begged you not to marry him because he wasn't a Christian? How your mother—" Aunt Mavis smiled sweetly. "—My dear little sister—she cried and warned you of the heartache that could come from marrying an unbeliever. It wasn't that they didn't like Bill, you know. We all liked him—I still do, of course. But, Rachel, it broke my heart—and your parents' hearts—to see you and Jennifer coming to church alone week after week. Thank God your dear parents aren't alive today to have to go through this!"

The reminder of the death of her parents in a car accident five years earlier cut Rachel deeply. She wasn't sure just how much more of this she could take. She knew Aunt Mavis meant well—and she knew she was probably right—but she just wasn't ready to hear it right now.

"I'm so glad you married such a nice Christian boy, Jenny," Aunt Mavis was saying. "Aren't you, Rachel?"

Rachel swallowed hard. "Of course I am, Aunt Mavis. But I just don't think this is the time . . . ."

Aunt Mavis raised her eyebrows. "Not the time for what, my dear? Have I said something to upset you?" Her face softened. "I certainly didn't mean to, Rachel. I only wanted to help."

"I know that, Aunt Mavis," Rachel answered, fighting the tears that were already stinging her eyelids. "I know. It's just that . . . I'm not up to praying right now. I know that sounds terrible, but . . . ."

Jennifer stood up and put her hand on her mother's shoulder.

"How about some coffee? I'll bet we could all use some."

Rachel looked up at her daughter gratefully. "Thank you, honey. I'd love some."

Snuffy jumped up and followed Jennifer into the kitchen. As soon as they'd gone, Aunt Mavis moved over onto the love seat and put her arm around Rachel. "I'm so sorry, my dear," she apologized. "I'm such a meddler! Just can't seem to learn when to keep my mouth shut!"

Rachel collapsed onto her aunt's soft shoulder and let the tears come. "That's a good girl," Aunt Mavis crooned. "Just let it all out. Go ahead and cry. That's what I'm here for, my dear. Just go ahead and have a good cry. We'll talk about it all later. There, there."

By the time Jennifer returned with three steaming mugs on a tray, Rachel felt she couldn't possibly cry anymore. Aunt Mavis handed her a handkerchief. Rachel wiped her eyes and blew her nose. Suddenly she sniffed the aroma of fresh coffee. She reached for a cup with trembling hands, sipping it slowly. "The coffee's delicious, Jenny," she smiled, savoring the rich taste. She took another sip and felt the warmth spreading through her.

"There's plenty more where that came from," Jennifer offered. "In fact, I was just thinking, maybe I should make some breakfast."

"Oh, no, I couldn't eat a thing!" Rachel protested.

"Of course you can." Aunt Mavis exclaimed. "Why, I don't know about you, but this running around at all hours of the morning has given me a huge appetite. Why don't you sit here with your mother, Jenny, and I'll go make breakfast. After all," she went on, standing up, "I may as well get used to where things are in the kitchen, since I plan on staying here for a while—at least until all this mess is straightened out, one way or the other."

Rachel and Jennifer stared after Aunt Mavis as she hurried out to the kitchen to attack her newfound mission. Then Rachel turned to her daughter. "Aunt Mavis is planning to stay here. Good grief, Jenny, what am I going to do?"

Jennifer shrugged and shook her head. "I have no idea, Mom. But you better think of something—quick! I think she's serious."

"I know she is," Rachel agreed.

"Maybe you could tell her you don't want to take her away from—"

"From what?" Rachel asked. "She's been retired for years. She lives alone in a small apartment on the other side of town. What would I take her away from? She doesn't even have a cat."

Jennifer brightened. "She has plants."

Rachel smiled at her daughter. "You know as well as I do what she'd say to that. After all, how long does it take to drive across Ventura twice a week to water plants? Who knows? The way Aunt Mavis is so big on physical fitness, maybe she'll jog over."

Jennifer giggled. "Oh, Mom, I love you."

"I know, sweetheart."

As the smell of bacon frying drifted into the living room, Aunt Mavis appeared in the doorway, her hands on her hips. "Well?" She raised her eyebrows. "Is anyone coming in to eat, or should I give it to the dog?"

Rachel stood up and took Jennifer's arm. "Let's go eat," she said and smiled.

"Are you sure, Mom?"

"Of course she's sure!" Aunt Mavis insisted. "Why, breakfast is the most important meal of the day. And as long as I'm doing the cooking around here, we'll have a good breakfast every morning."

Aunt Mavis turned to lead the way. Rachel and Jennifer looked at each other and rolled their eyes, as they followed Aunt Mavis obediently into the kitchen.

Chapter 3

The hot Santa Ana winds that had blown all week had finally died down and Rachel, Jennifer, and Aunt Mavis were sitting in the lounge chairs beside the pool, as Snuffy dozed in the shade nearby. The late September sun was warm, and the glare of the pool caused Rachel to cover her eyes with her arm, even though she was wearing sunglasses. The low drone of conversation between Jennifer and Aunt Mavis grew fainter, until images of Bill began floating through Rachel's mind—a young Bill, laughing, handsome, tossing a baby up in the air and catching her as she squealed with delight—but why was the baby blond? Jennifer never had blond hair. Rachel awoke with a jump, feeling confused and panicked.

"Sorry, Mom. I didn't mean to startle you." Rachel blinked and squinted up at the stocky figure standing over her, his hand on her shoulder. She couldn't see his face, but his golden hair glistened in the sun.

"Chuck." Rachel smiled as he bent to kiss her cheek. "I'm so glad you're here."

Snuffy had come over to greet Chuck, who patted him briefly. "Hello, old boy." He turned back to Rachel and pulled up a chair next to hers. Snuffy went back to his spot under the orange tree.

"I'm sorry I couldn't come sooner, Mom. I had a few things to get squared away first."

Rachel reached over and squeezed his hand. "I understand. Please don't worry about me." She looked over at Jennifer and Aunt Mavis. "As you can see, I've been well taken care of."

Chuck grinned. "It certainly looks that way."

Jennifer arched her eyebrows and looked at her husband. "Aunt Mavis is planning to stay here with Mom for a while," she informed him.

"Wonderful!" Chuck responded heartily. "I think that's a great idea, Aunt Mavis."

Jennifer glanced at her mother, but Rachel did not react.

"Thank you, my dear!" Aunt Mavis was beaming. "I always said you were such a sensible boy. As a matter of fact, if you and Jenny are going to be here for a while, I believe I'll just run over to my place and pick up some things. I won't be long."

"Take your time, Aunt Mavis. We won't be going home until sometime this evening. In fact, I had wondered if Jenny shouldn't stay here with her mother, but since you'll be here, I don't suppose that will be necessary." Chuck looked over at Jennifer. "What do you think, Jen?"

Jennifer shrugged uncertainly. "Well, I . . . ."

"Of course she doesn't need to stay!" Aunt Mavis interrupted. "Why, you two don't need to worry about a thing. I'll take good care of everything here. Rachel and I will be just fine, won't we, my dear?"

Everyone stared at Rachel. This was her last chance to be rid of Aunt Mavis. She took a deep breath. "Yes, Aunt Mavis and I will be fine. Jennifer, you go on home with your husband."

Aunt Mavis slapped her hands against her thighs, and smiled. "Well, then, everything's settled." She stood up abruptly. "I'm off to pick up my things. You three just sit here and relax. I'll be back in plenty of time to fix dinner."

Aunt Mavis had no sooner gone back into the house than Jennifer turned to her husband. "Chuck, I wish you hadn't encouraged Aunt Mavis that way."

Chuck blinked and tilted his head to one side. "Why not? Mom needs someone here with her right now, and Aunt Mavis is perfect. What's the problem?"

Jennifer shook her head and sighed. "Oh, Chuck, sometimes! Honey, I know you think Aunt Mavis is just great, but can you imagine what it would be like to live with her? Why do you suppose she never married? I know she means well, but she's always butting in where it's none of her business."

"Aren't you being a little hard on her, Jen?" Chuck asked softly. "After all, she only wants to help."

"Chuck's right," Rachel interrupted.

Jennifer jerked her head toward her mother.

"It's true," Rachel went on. "I know she can be a pain in the neck sometimes, but she's always been there everytime any of us needed her. And you know something? I think right now I do need her. I just didn't realize it until a few minutes ago."

Jennifer shook her head again. "I don't know, Mom."

"Trust me, Jenny." Rachel forced a smile. "Aunt Mavis and I will be just fine."

* * *

After an early dinner, Chuck volunteered to do the dishes.

"I'll help," Jennifer added, jumping up to clear the table.

"Wonderful!" Aunt Mavis added, looking over at Rachel. "That will give Rachel and me a chance to take Snuffy for a walk."

"A walk!" Rachel exclaimed, almost knocking over her water glass. "Snuffy? You must be kidding! Snuffy is terrible on a leash. All he does is run. We'd never keep up with him."

Aunt Mavis's blue eyes twinkled. "Oh, I wouldn't be so sure about that. You do know where his leash is, don't you?"

"Well, sure, but . . . ."

"Well, then, get some comfortable shoes on and let's go."

Aunt Mavis was whistling as they headed out the door, Snuffy was barking and running in circles, tangling his leash around Rachel's legs, and Rachel was praying the walk would be a very short one.

As they started down the street, Aunt Mavis took the lead. Snuffy was only too eager to keep up with her, while Rachel half-ran, half-stumbled along behind, trying desperately to hold on to Snuffy's leash.

"Come along, dear," Aunt Mavis called back. "The streetlights are already on, and it will be dark soon."

Rachel tried to pick up her pace, but only succeeded in tripping over Snuffy. She caught herself before she fell, but her teeth came down hard on her tongue. "Darn it!" she muttered, as she tasted the warm, salty blood.

"Did you say something, my dear?" Aunt Mavis asked, turning back to look at Rachel.

Rachel shook her head, sucking her sore tongue. "No, Aunt Mavis," she managed to answer. "I didn't say a thing."

Aunt Mavis smiled and resumed her pace.

After about ten minutes, Rachel decided she couldn't go any farther. "Aunt Mavis!" she gasped. "I can't go on! I've got to stop and rest!"

"Nonsense!" Aunt Mavis said without breaking her stride. "When you get to be my age, then you can think about resting!"

With you around, I'll never live that long! Rachel thought, straining to hang on to Snuffy.

By the time they finally reached home, Rachel was exhausted.

"Wasn't that fun?" Aunt Mavis asked, as they walked in the front door. "Why, you look better already! There's nothing like a nice brisk walk to put some color in your cheeks!"

Rachel stared at her aunt, too out of breath to answer. She took Snuffy's leash and hung it up in the hall closet, wincing at the sight of Bill's raincoat hanging next to hers. She closed the closet door quickly.

"Well," Aunt Mavis smiled, as Rachel turned toward her, "I believe I'll go see if there's any iced tea left. Would you care for some, my dear?"

Rachel nodded gratefully, as Snuffy came back in from the kitchen with fresh drops of water dripping from his mouth. He sprawled out on his stomach on the cool tile of the entryway, panting heavily.

"I know just how you feel, Snuf," Rachel whispered. Chuck and Jennifer must be sitting out on the patio, she thought, walking toward the den. The sliding glass door was open, and Rachel could hear voices outside.

She stopped at the door as she heard Chuck say, "I don't know, Jen. I think we should tell her."

"How can we, Chuck?" Jennifer asked. "How can we tell her this on top of everything else?"

Rachel hadn't turned on any lights in the den, and she stood, frozen in the darkness, knowing she should say something to let them know she was there, but unable to open her mouth. What was it they were keeping from her?

"I think you're wrong," Chuck went on. "A little good news right now might be just what she needs."

"Chuck, any other time this would be good news, but how do you think Mom is going to feel when she realizes that Dad is going to become a grandfather, as well as a father? I think we should give her a little more time to get used to the situation with Dad and Sheryl before we tell her about our baby. Besides, things with Dad could change."

The lights shimmering on the pool seemed to hypnotize Rachel, as once again she felt herself floating high above her body, watching and hearing everything as if she were far, far away.

Suddenly the room was full of light and Rachel jumped, as she heard the tinkle of ice against glass. She spun around to see Aunt Mavis walking toward her with a pitcher of iced tea and glasses on a tray.

"Well, there you are!" Aunt Mavis exclaimed. "What in the world were you doing standing there in the dark? Let's go outside and join the party."

* * *

Rachel sat down stiffly, while Aunt Mavis poured the tea.

"Well, how was your walk, Mom?" Chuck asked.

Rachel looked at him. Did he know she had been listening?

"Mom?"

Rachel turned to look at her daughter.

"Mom, are you all right?"

She always frowns so when she's worried, Rachel thought.

Jennifer reached out and put her hand on Rachel's arm. "Mom?"

Rachel shook her head. "I'm sorry, darling. What did you say?"

Jennifer and Chuck looked at each other. Chuck cleared his throat. "We just wondered how you enjoyed your walk."

"Oh, the walk." Rachel smiled absently. "The walk was fine. Just fine."

"It certainly was," Aunt Mavis agreed, handing Rachel a glass of iced tea. "Of course, once you're used to taking them, we'll be able to go much farther! I usually walk at least three miles several times a week. Exercise and diet are so important. Don't you agree, Chuck?"

Chuck grinned. "You bet, Aunt Mavis!"

"So," Aunt Mavis continued, "how are things going at your new church?"

"Things are going well," Chuck answered. "It's a small congregation—less than a hundred—but the people are so friendly, and so receptive to a new pastor! I was a little concerned about that at first. The last pastor they had was there for quite a while, and was loved and respected by everyone, so it's a little difficult to fill his shoes. But I'm doing the best I can!"

"You'll do wonderfully!" Aunt Mavis exclaimed. "Why, you'll have them eating out of your hand in no time."

Chuck laughed. "Well, I don't know about that."

Jennifer got up and stood behind her husband's chair. She put her hands on his shoulders and bent down and kissed the top of his head. "Aunt Mavis is right, you know. After all, you're a great pastor."

Chuck reached up and took one of Jennifer's hands and kissed it. Then he looked over at Rachel. "Mom," he began, "I hate to be the one to break this up, but maybe we should get going. I need to go over my sermon, and since we came in separate cars, I don't want Jenny driving too late at night, after getting up so early and all." He stopped, his face turning red.

"It's all right," Rachel assured him. "I know you're all trying to keep the conversation away from Bill and me, especially since I explained the circumstances to you earlier. But it's something we have to face. At this very moment. . . ." She swallowed hard and took a deep breath. Her voice dropped a notch. "At this very moment, he's probably holding another woman in his arms—a woman who is going to have his child. There's no way of avoiding the truth, so please don't try. I've got to learn to deal with it. I'm just so thankful to all of you for your love and support. But, please, don't feel badly about going. You two have things you need to do. Aunt Mavis will be here with me." She glanced at her aunt and smiled briefly. "We'll be fine, I promise."

Jennifer took her hands from Chuck's shoulders, and walked over to her mother. She bent over and put her arms around her and kissed her cheek. "I love you, Mom."

"I love you, too, darling," Rachel answered, patting Jennifer's hand. "Now, you two get home and get some rest, you hear?"

Jennifer nodded. "All right. But I'll call you tomorrow, okay?"

"And you call us if you need anything, Mom," Chuck added, standing up. "Anything at all."

Rachel looked at Chuck and Jennifer standing side by side, and smiled. Chuck was slightly self-conscious about the fact that Jennifer was two inches taller than he was. Jennifer insisted that it didn't bother her, but she had started wearing flat shoes soon after she and Chuck began dating.

"I'll call," Rachel promised, moving to stand up.

"Oh, don't get up, Mom!" Chuck said quickly. "You and Aunt Mavis just sit here and relax." He turned to Aunt Mavis. "Thanks for everything."

Aunt Mavis winked at him. "Preach a good one tomorrow."

Chuck grinned and saluted.

Jennifer blew Aunt Mavis a kiss, then turned to look at her mother once again. "Good night, Mom."

"Good night, sweetheart."

Rachel sighed as they left and stared at her drink, swirling the iced tea around absently.

"More iced tea?" Aunt Mavis asked.

Rachel looked at her aunt blankly.

Aunt Mavis held up the pitcher of tea and repeated her offer. "Would you care for a little more tea, my dear?"

"Oh, no thanks, Aunt Mavis."

"You didn't eat much dinner," Aunt Mavis went on. "Would you care for some fruit or something?"

Rachel shook her head. "No, nothing, thanks. I'm just not very hungry."

Aunt Mavis's eyes lit up. "How about a swim? It's still early."

"No, Aunt Mavis," Rachel answered firmly. "I don't want to swim, either. I just want to sit here for a while, all right?"

"Certainly, dear. Do you mind if I sit here with you or would you rather be alone?"

"Oh, no," Rachel answered quickly. "No, I don't want to be alone. Please stay."

Aunt Mavis leaned back in her chair. They sat in the stillness of the warm evening, watching the lights play on the water and listening to an agitated dog barking somewhere in the distance.

After a few moments, Aunt Mavis looked up at Rachel and asked, "Well, which service do you want to go to in the morning? I usually go to the early service, as you know, but if you'd care to sleep in—"

"Go to whichever one you prefer," Rachel interrupted. "I'm not going."

Aunt Mavis blinked and stared at her niece. "I can't remember the last time you missed church, Rachel. Why aren't you going?"

Rachel closed her eyes. "I'm just not, that's all."

"But you must have a reason, dear," Aunt Mavis persisted.

Rachel didn't answer.

Aunt Mavis pulled her chair closer to Rachel's. She pursed her lips and squinted her eyes. "Rachel," she began, "church is exactly where you need to be right now."

Rachel opened her eyes and looked at her aunt. "No, Aunt Mavis. I don't need to be there, and I'm not going."

They stared at each other in silence, until Aunt Mavis asked, "Is it because you don't want to face anyone? If it is, you shouldn't feel that way, you know. They're your family, too. They care about you." She put her hand on Rachel's arm. "And so do I."

"I know you do, Aunt Mavis," Rachel whispered, struggling to fight back the tears. "I know you do, but I'm not going to church, and that's final! Please, Aunt Mavis, I just don't want to talk about it anymore."

"But, Rachel," Aunt Mavis argued, "you need to be with other believers. You need to be praying and reading the Word. You need to draw your strength from God now as never before!"

Rachel sat up straight, her face determined. "What I need," she said slowly, "is for everyone to leave me alone and mind their own business!"

Aunt Mavis didn't answer. Suddenly Rachel began to cry. "Oh, Aunt Mavis, I'm so sorry! I didn't mean that. Truly I didn't."

"I know you didn't. I know that, dear. It's all right. I understand."

"No, Aunt Mavis," Rachel said, crying softly. "You don't understand. How could you? You've never even been married." She groaned, then buried her head in her hands. "Oh, Aunt Mavis, please forgive me!"

"There's nothing to forgive, my dear. You may be right, you know. Maybe I don't understand." She lowered her voice almost to a whisper. "But Jesus does. And he loves you, Rachel."

Rachel's head snapped up and she glared at her aunt. Then she jumped up and stared down at her, her fists clenched at her sides. "Jesus understands, does he? Well, if he's so understanding and so loving, why did he let this happen? Why didn't he stop it? If he cares so much about me, why is my husband off somewhere making love to another woman? Why, Aunt Mavis?

Can you answer me that?"

There were tears in Aunt Mavis's eyes, too, as she stared silently at her niece. After a moment, she stood up in front of Rachel and looked directly into her eyes. "I know you're terribly hurt, my dear. And I know nothing seems fair or right. But God can work all this out, Rachel, if you'll just let him. He wants to help you."

"What's He going to do, Aunt Mavis?" Rachel asked sarcastically. "Is he going to bring Bill back home? Will he give him a change of heart? Make him repent? Well, let me tell you something. I don't care if Bill comes crawling back here on his knees, begging to come home, I will never take him back. And I will never forgive him. Never!"

Aunt Mavis grabbed Rachel's arms gently. "Rachel, listen to me. Jesus died for Bill, too, you know. He loves him just as much as he loves you and me. And if God can forgive us, we must be willing to forgive, as well."

Rachel's eyes narrowed and her jaw muscles twitched. "I used to believe that, Aunt Mavis," she answered, her voice cold and hard. "But now I know there are some things that even God doesn't forgive."

Chapter 4

Rachel winced at each sharp snip of the scissors, as she watched the wet strands of hair fall to the floor around her. It had taken her two weeks to get up the nerve to call for an appointment, but once she had, she was determined to be rid of the long, heavy hair that had weighed her down for years. She closed her eyes, remembering how much Bill had loved her long hair when they were first married. He never tired of running his fingers through its thick, soft silkiness. The one time she had mentioned getting it cut, he became so upset she had dropped the subject. However, when she began wearing her hair pulled back off her face in a tight bun at the back of her neck, insisting she was getting too old for long, straight hair, Bill had suggested she get it cut, maybe curled. He had said it might make her look younger. She had refused, stubbornly wearing it pulled back for the next twelve years. But from then on, when she took her hair down at night, Bill no longer touched it or told her how beautiful it was.

"Mrs. Webster?"

Rachel jumped and her eyes flew open.

"Sorry if I startled you, Mrs. Webster. I just wondered how you wanted the sides. Is this short enough?"

Rachel squinted at the hairdresser, then blinked as she looked in the mirror. Her head felt light. She touched the back of her neck, then took a deep breath. "Yes. Yes, this will be fine, Doreen."

Doreen smiled. "Great! Well, let's start rolling you up!"

Rachel blinked again, puzzled, then realized Doreen was talking about the permanent Rachel had asked for. "Something short, simple, and easy to take care of," had been her instructions.

Rachel leaned back in her chair and tried to relax as Doreen began dividing what was left of Rachel's hair into sections. She had told no one of her plans to have her hair cut, and she wondered what everyone would think.

The bell on the shop door tinkled as someone walked in, but Rachel's back was to the door and she couldn't see who it was. The hairdresser who had been sitting in the chair next to Rachel, absently filing her nails, stood up. "Hi, Joan. I'm all ready for you. Have a seat."

Rachel's eyes widened as she realized it was her pastor's wife, Joan Mitchell, who was sitting down in the chair next to her. Joan had called Rachel twice over the last three weeks since Bill left, but both times Aunt Mavis had taken a message, and Rachel had not returned the calls.

"Rachel?" Joan had spotted her. She leaned closer. "I hardly recognized you! Your hair!"

Rachel tried to smile. "I decided to have it cut."

Joan sat back and nodded her head slowly. "So I see." She hesitated, as if wondering what to say next, but just then her hairdresser called her to the sink.

While Joan was having her hair washed, Rachel squirmed. How could she possibly have picked the same shop and the same day to have her hair done as Joan? Was this Joan's regular hairdresser? If only Doreen would work a little faster!

Doreen was only half done rolling Rachel's hair when Joan got up from the chair at the sink, holding a towel around her wet hair. As Joan walked back to her chair, Rachel's heart beat faster. Surely she wouldn't bring up anything here, among all these strangers. Rachel clasped her sweaty palms together.

Joan smiled as she sat down. "So, Rachel, how are you? We've missed you at church."

"I . . . ." Rachel swallowed. "I meant to call you back, Joan, but . . . ."

Joan looked concerned. "I just wanted to make sure everything was all right." She raised an eyebrow slightly.

Rachel pretended to be watching Doreen's progress in the mirror. "Everything's fine," she mumbled, trying to sound casual. "I've just been busy."

"Well, I'm sure that's true," Joan persisted, "but, you see, I'm really in sort of a bind. You remember Lynne Woods, don't you? The young woman who's been teaching the four- and five-year-old Sunday school class?" She didn't wait for Rachel to answer. "Well, her husband got a new job down in the Los Angeles area, and they're moving next month. You taught that class for several years, didn't you?"

Rachel reddened. "Oh, well, that was a long time ago, when Jennifer was little."

"You'd be perfect for it, Rachel," Joan went on. "And you know how hard it is to get Sunday school teachers—especially good ones! You'd be doing me a favor."

Rachel shook her head. "No. I mean, I couldn't. I just don't think this is a good time." Rachel looked at Joan pleadingly. Couldn't she understand? Was she going to make her spell out the reasons?

Joan shrugged. "Well, I don't want to push you. But if you change your mind, I'd really be grateful."

Rachel didn't answer. She closed her eyes again, hoping to end the conversation.

"You want the usual, I assume?" Joan's hairdresser was asking pleasantly.

"Yes, Marie, thank you," Joan answered. So this is her regular hairdresser, Rachel thought. She made a mental note to change beauty shops.

"It just seems such a waste—all your experience working with kids and teaching Sunday school."

Rachel opened her eyes when she realized Joan was once again speaking to her. "Excuse me?"

"Oh, I was just thinking about all the years you spent teaching

Sunday school and leading girls' club when Jennifer was little. It just seems such a shame to waste all that talent and experience."

Joan sighed. "This is my only morning off during the week, now that I've taken over as director of the church preschool. We have a Monday/Wednesday class, and a Tuesday/Thursday class, but nothing on Friday, so that's the day I get my hair done. I don't know what I'm going to do when Lynne leaves next month. Did you know she's been working as a morning aide at the preschool, as well as teaching the Sunday school class? So, as well as a replacement for Sundays, I've got to find a new aide for Tuesday and Thursday mornings, too. I've got Mondays and Wednesdays covered, but . . . ."

Joan's voice droned on, as Rachel tried to glance at her watch without being too obvious. How much longer would she have to sit here listening to this?

"There!" Doreen exclaimed, patting the last curl into place. "Here, Mrs. Webster, why don't you hold this towel over your face for a minute, and I'll put the solution on. Then you'll be ready to sit under the dryer."

Thank goodness! Rachel thought, putting the towel over her eyes and nose. The solution smelled terrible, as it trickled down the back of her neck through the cotton ring Doreen had placed around Rachel's curlers. She was beginning to have trouble breathing when Doreen announced, "Okay, Mrs. Webster, let's go put you under the dryer for a few minutes."

Rachel jumped up and hurried to the dryer. She knew Joan was watching her. The dryer was hot and uncomfortable, but the noise was a good excuse for not carrying on a conversation. She picked up a magazine from the stand beside the dryer and flipped through it absently.

Before long, Doreen was back, lifting the dryer hood and checking Rachel's curls. "They look great. Let's go rinse you off and see what we've got."

By the time the curlers were out and Rachel was back in her chair, Marie had almost finished Joan's hair. Rachel thought it didn't look any different than when she had come in.

"Oh, Rachel," Joan exclaimed, looking up at her, "your hair is darling! Are you going to leave it nice and curly like that?"

Rachel had been so busy looking at Joan's hair, she had forgotten about her own. She looked in the mirror and gasped. Was that her? There were short, wet, bouncy curls all over her head! It's what she'd asked for, but somehow she hadn't imagined that her entire face would change.

"Yes," she heard herself saying. "I'm going to leave it just like this."

"Good for you, Mrs. Webster!" Doreen smiled. "It makes you look ten years younger!"

Rachel stood up. "Thank you, Doreen. How much do I owe you?"

"I'll go write up your bill."

"Rachel," Joan said hurriedly, "before you leave, I just want to ask you to think about what we talked about, will you? About the Sunday school class?" She brightened suddenly. "Or maybe even the aide's position? It might work out very well for you, now that you have so much time on your hands and—" Joan stopped, her cheeks flushed.

Rachel fumbled in her purse for her wallet and keys. "I'll think about it, Joan. Good-bye."

* * *

"Oh, my dear! What in the . . . ."

"Do you like it, Aunt Mavis?" Rachel asked, turning slowly.

Aunt Mavis, holding an unopened can of tuna in one hand, reached out and touched Rachel's hair. "It's so soft. And so curly."

Rachel frowned. "Do you think it's too curly, Aunt Mavis?"

Aunt Mavis stepped back and looked at her niece. "I think it's perfect," she announced. "Just perfect."

"Really, Aunt Mavis?"

"Really! Oh, my dear, I can't tell you how many times I've

thought how nice you'd look with a new hairstyle, but I had no idea! Why, you look five years younger."

Rachel grinned. "My hairdresser said ten years."

Aunt Mavis squinted her eyes and walked around Rachel again. "She's right. Ten years—definitely ten years."

They laughed, then Rachel asked, "Do you really like it, Aunt Mavis?"

"I really like it, Rachel. Very much."

"Joan liked it, too," Rachel said, immediately wishing she hadn't mentioned it.

"Joan? Joan Mitchell?"

Rachel nodded and cleared her throat. "She, uh, was having her hair done the same time I was."

Aunt Mavis raised her eyebrows. "Joan has her hair done?" She grinned. "Somehow I thought her hair just came sort of pre-packaged, you know? I don't think I've ever seen one hair on her head out of place since I've known her."

"Don't worry," Rachel smiled. "She didn't change anything." She sat down at the kitchen table, and Aunt Mavis sat down next to her.

"So, what else did Joan have to say, besides that she liked your hair? You never did call her back, did you?"

Rachel shook her head. "I'm afraid not, Aunt Mavis. I just didn't feel like talking to her, I guess. And I certainly wish I hadn't run into her today. She asked me to take over the four- and five-year-old Sunday school class when Lynne Woods and her husband leave next month."

"Why, that's wonderful!" Aunt Mavis beamed. "That would be just perfect for you. I'm so anxious to see you get involved at church again. I've been so worried—"

"I'm not taking the class, Aunt Mavis," Rachel interrupted. "I just don't want to make any commitments right now. Besides, if I said yes to that, the next thing you know she'd be trying to talk me into taking the aide's position on Tuesday and Thursday mornings at the preschool."

Aunt Mavis sat up straight. "There's a position open at the preschool? Oh, Rachel, that's exactly what you need. I think you do have too much time on your hands these days . . . ."

"That's exactly what Joan said. Aunt Mavis, why can't you and Joan and Jennifer and Chuck and— everyone—just leave me alone! Why does everyone else seem to know exactly what I need to do with my life? Maybe I just want to sit around here and do nothing. It's my life, isn't it?"

Aunt Mavis put her hand on Rachel's. "Of course it is, my dear. But we all love you. We're so sorry that you've been hurt, and we want to help you find some direction for yourself."

"And you think all it takes is teaching Sunday school or preschool a few hours a week to get everything together again?"

"It could help," Aunt Mavis answered softly. "And you know how much you've always loved children. When you were a little girl, all you ever talked about was growing up to be a teacher like your Aunt Mavis someday. Why not now?"

Rachel opened her mouth to answer, but the look in Aunt Mavis's pale blue eyes stopped her. It was true. Rachel did love kids. She had always wanted to be a teacher. And she had realized over the past couple of weeks that if she didn't start getting out of the house more often, she was going to go crazy.

She sighed. "All right. I'll call Joan—later. I'll talk to her about it, but no promises, okay?"

Aunt Mavis clapped her hands together. "Wonderful! Oh, Rachel, that's just wonderful. I'm so glad." Her eyes opened wide. "Let's forget this tuna and go out to lunch somewhere and celebrate."

"I can't, Aunt Mavis. Not today." She looked down at her hands and twisted her wedding ring nervously. "There's something I have to take care of first."

* * *

The sun was warm, but the stiff breeze reminded Rachel that fall had arrived, as she stepped out of the sleek, gray Thunderbird and self-consciously patted her curly hair. She clutched her purse under her arm, smoothed her navy blue skirt, and walked determinedly across the parking lot and through the double doors. She glanced at the directory on the wall, found the name she was looking for, and pushed the elevator button. Then she changed her mind. It's only on the second floor, she told herself. The walk will do me good.

She took a deep breath and started up the stairs. Reading the office numbers as she reached the top, she turned left. Two doors down, she stopped, her hand frozen as she reached for the door-knob. Light-headed, she stood, unmoving, as the familiar buzzing began in her ears.

The elevator door slid open behind her, and she jumped as she realized someone was getting off. Shaking her head and trying to concentrate, she opened the door and stepped into the spacious, immaculate office. There were three chairs and a couch spaced evenly around the room, with several magazines lined up neatly on a coffee table in front of the couch. An elderly man sat in one of the chairs, reading the newspaper. He lowered the paper and glanced up at Rachel. She smiled nervously, but he ignored her and went back to his paper.

As she closed the door, a small glass window slid open across the room from her and a voice asked, "May I help you?"

Rachel walked hesitantly toward the window. A tiny woman about Rachel's age looked up at her. Rachel didn't speak.

"May I help you?" the woman repeated.

"Yes, I, uh . . . ." Rachel cleared her throat and tried again. "I'm Rachel Webster. I have a two-thirty appointment with—"

"Of course," the woman interrupted with a smile. "Mrs. Webster. Sit down, please. He'll be with you in just a few moments. Would you like some coffee?"

Rachel shook her head. "I don't believe so, thank you." She turned and sat down stiffly in the nearest chair, then realized there were no magazines near her. Should she get back up and get one off the coffee table? The receptionist had said he would only be a few minutes. She'd wait.

The door opened and a tall, attractive woman with very red hair walked in. She moved confidently to the receptionist's window, which was closed again, and rapped on it impatiently.

The window slid open. "Yes? Oh, hello, Mrs. Reed."

"Tell George I'm here, will you?"

"I don't believe you have an appointment, do you, Mrs. Reed?"

The red-haired woman leaned over and repeated huskily, "Just tell him I'm here. He'll see me."

She turned and walked over to the couch, plunking down with a disgusted sigh, as the receptionist's window slammed shut.

The old man had lowered his paper again, and seemed much more interested in the red-haired woman than he had been in Rachel. He stared at her openly, until the woman looked over at him and smiled. "Like what you see, old man?" She raised her skirt a couple of inches, then laughed when he blushed and hid behind his paper again.

Rachel stared at her hands folded in her lap and wished she had accepted the receptionist's offer of coffee, or had at least picked up a magazine. She knew the woman was looking at her. She heard her take something out of her purse.

"Got a light?"

Rachel looked up, confused. The old man was still reading his paper. The woman held out her cigarette. "I need a light," she repeated, looking directly at Rachel.

"I don't smoke. I'm sorry," Rachel answered, immediately annoyed with herself for apologizing. She was glad the woman didn't have a light. Rachel hated cigarette smoke.

"I have a match," the old man offered.

"Why, thank you." The woman smiled exaggeratedly, then held the cigarette to her lips and raised her eyebrows. The old man got up and lit it for her, then went back to his chair. She took a long, deep drag, then exhaled in Rachel's direction, smiling slightly.

The phone rang and Rachel heard the receptionist's voice. "Langsford and Jordan. May I help you?"

As the receptionist finished her phone conversation, Rachel pretended to be looking for something in her purse, trying to avoid the red-haired woman's gaze and trying desperately not to cough, as the acrid smell of smoke began to burn her throat and nostrils. Suddenly the door to the inner offices opened.

"Mrs. Webster?"

Rachel looked up at the receptionist. She was standing at the door, smiling at her.

"Mrs. Webster, Mr. Langsford will see you now."

"What about me?" the red-haired woman asked. "I need to see George."

"Mr. Jordan will be with you as soon as he can," the receptionist assured her.

Rachel jumped up, almost spilling the contents of her purse. She hurried past the receptionist, noticing again how tiny she was, and feeling a little guilty for leaving the old man alone with the red-haired woman.

"I'm Sylvia," the receptionist said. She lowered her voice to a whisper. "I hope Mrs. Reed didn't give you any problems. She's not one of our favorite clients."

Rachel smiled and shook her head. "No. No problem."

Sylvia opened a heavy wooden door and announced, "Mr. Langsford, Mrs. Webster is here to see you."

A tall, heavyset man with a receding hairline stood up and walked around to the front of his desk, his large, meaty hand extended in welcome. "Mrs. Webster," he smiled warmly, "come in." His handshake was firm and strong, and Rachel liked him right away.

"Sit down, please." He indicated a large, comfortable chair in front of his desk. It wasn't until she sank down into the softness of the chair that Rachel realized how weak and shaky she felt.

Mr. Langsford poured a cup of black coffee from the pot behind his desk and handed it to her. She was glad he hadn't asked if she wanted any, or whether she took cream or sugar. She didn't feel capable of making any more decisions at the moment.

He sat back down behind his desk and leaned forward, folding his hands in front of him. "Now, Mrs. Webster, how can I help you?"

Rachel took a sip of the hot black coffee, holding it in her mouth for a moment. Then she swallowed and looked directly into Mr. Langsford's soft, gray eyes.

"Mr. Langsford, I need your help. I want a divorce. My husband has left me for another woman, and I want him to pay for it."

Chapter 5

"Miss Rachel, can you tie my shoe?"

Rachel looked down into the upturned face of a towheaded four-year-old whose soft brown eyes looked too big for the rest of him. The name on his shirt read, "Hi! I'm Jeremy." His nose was running.

"I tell you what, Jeremy," Rachel smiled, as she pulled a tissue from her apron pocket. "I'll help you tie your shoe if you'll blow your nose."

Jeremy shrugged. "I don't know how to blow my nose."

Rachel knelt down beside him. "Then I guess I'll help you with two things. Here, hold the tissue like this. Good. Now, take a deep breath and blow. Hey, I thought you said you didn't know how to blow your nose! That was very good! Come on, let's try it one more time. Then we'll work on your shoe."

By the time they had the shoelace safely double-knotted, Rachel's legs were beginning to cramp. But before she could stand up, Jeremy threw his arms around her neck. "You're a nice teacher, Miss Rachel. I wish I could have you for a grandma!"

Jeremy ran off to rejoin the other children playing in the sandbox, as Rachel stood up stiffly, tears filling her eyes. "Not here, Lord," she whispered. "Please don't let me cry here!"

She took a deep breath and blinked the tears from her eyes, as she looked around the sunbathed playground. Children seemed to be everywhere, running, climbing, laughing, squealing. Although Rachel's position was actually that of an aide, she loved it when the children called her "Teacher."

In the far corner of the playground, sitting on a bench beside

48

the swings, sat Susan Frost—"Miss Susan"—the teacher of the four-year-olds. She was young and vibrant, and Rachel enjoyed working with her almost as much as she enjoyed working with the children.

When Rachel had first called Joan the day after they talked at the beauty shop, she'd only expected to ask her a few questions about the job. She'd never dreamed Joan would talk her into starting work the following Tuesday. But Rachel had been firm in turning down Joan's pleas for a Sunday school teacher, insisting she was only taking the aide's position on a trial basis.

Now, only two weeks later, at the end of her fourth morning at work, Rachel knew she had found her niche. She had even talked to Susan to find out what courses she would have to take to become a licensed pre-school teacher. She had been pleasantly surprised to find that she could take all the necessary courses at the community college in town. Although she was too late to get in on the fall semester, she planned to sign up for as many classes as possible the next semester.

Susan's head was bent as she read a book to a small group of children gathered around her on the bench. Her long dark hair spilled down in front of her, shining in the sun as she read. Tucking it back behind her ear, she closed the book and looked up. She waved at Rachel, motioning her to join them. Susan's really not pretty until she smiles, Rachel thought, walking over toward the group on the bench. Then she reminds me so much of Jenny.

"Hi!" Susan called. "How's it going?"

"Fine," Rachel answered. "I'm really enjoying it so far."

Susan grinned. "You're a natural. And I know the kids love you." She turned to the little girl on her left. "Isn't that right, Crystal?"

Crystal nodded enthusiastically, her short curls bouncing in agreement. "I love you, Miss Rachel."

"So do I," another child piped up.

"Me, too."

"Me, too!"

Rachel swallowed the lump in her throat. She didn't trust herself to answer.

Susan laughed. "You see? It's unanimous." She glanced in the direction of the sandbox. "And it's pretty obvious how Jeremy feels. When he arrived this morning before you did, the first thing out of his mouth was, 'Where's Miss Rachel?' You've made quite an impression."

Rachel wasn't sure her legs would hold her up much longer. She sat down on the bench next to Crystal. "I'm very happy here," she said softly.

* * *

Aunt Mavis threw open the front door and she and Rachel hurried in, laughing breathlessly. Snuffy, like Rachel, had grown accustomed to their evening walks and no longer returned home exhausted. Barking excitedly, he bounded into the kitchen for a drink of water, his toenails clicking across the tiled floor. "Oh, Aunt Mavis," Rachel chuckled, shaking her head as she hung up Snuffy's leash, "I'd forgotten some of those wonderful stories of yours from your teaching days! You used to tell me about the funny things some of your students did, but I guess I never really appreciated them until now. Aren't kids wonderful?"

Aunt Mavis smiled as they walked into the den. "You really like your new job, don't you, my dear?"

Rachel sat down on the couch next to her aunt. "I love it! The people I work with are so nice. And the kids! Oh, I wish you could see Jeremy! They're all great kids; but Jeremy—there's something so special about that little guy."

Aunt Mavis nodded. "I know exactly what you mean. There's always one like that. And you know something? You never really forget them. Even now, after all these years, there are certain children that I still think of and wonder about, even pray for. I'll probably never see or hear from them again, but I like to think they're happy and well. I often wonder if any of them ever think of me."

Rachel laughed again. "How could anyone ever forget you, Aunt Mavis?"

Aunt Mavis smiled, her eyes twinkling. "I suppose you're right, my dear." She stood up abruptly. "Well, how about a fire? We haven't lit one yet this year, and tomorrow's the last day of October. I've noticed a chill in the air in the evenings lately, haven't you?"

Rachel nodded. "A fire would be nice. Have we got enough kindling?"

"Plenty," Aunt Mavis assured her. "Want to help?"

The fire was soon blazing and Aunt Mavis and Rachel settled back on the couch, gazing into the orange flames.

"I'm glad you talked me into having the chimney sweep out last week," Rachel commented. "I never would have thought of that. Bill always took care of those things before."

Her voice trailed off and they were quiet again, listening to the crackling and popping of the fire. Aunt Mavis reached over and put her hand on Rachel's.

The doorbell made them both jump. "I wonder who that could be," Rachel said, moving to get up.

Aunt Mavis patted Rachel's hand. "Sit still, my dear. I'll get it."

Rachel smiled when she heard Chuck's and Jennifer's voices. She jumped up to greet them.

"Hi, Mom," Jennifer called, walking into the den and throwing her arms around her mother. "Surprise!" She kissed Rachel's cheek.

"It certainly is," Rachel agreed. "A very nice surprise."

Aunt Mavis and Chuck walked in arm-in-arm. "Look who I found!" Aunt Mavis announced.

Rachel hugged her son-in-law. "Yes," she smiled again. "Isn't it wonderful?"

"Oh, a fire!" Jennifer looked at her husband. "I think we got here just in time." She hurried over to the fireplace and sat down on the raised hearth, holding her hands out to warm them. "Mmm, that feels good. It's getting chilly outside."

"You know Jenny," Chuck teased. "She thinks anything under seventy degrees is cold."

He sat down on the couch between Rachel and Aunt Mavis. Snuffy had come in from the kitchen and was lying in front of the fireplace at Jennifer's feet, as Jennifer stroked him lovingly. Rachel looked at her daughter, her hair hanging loosely down her shoulders and back, her cheeks pink from the cool night air, and thought again how very beautiful she was. Glancing at Chuck, Rachel knew from the look on his face as he watched his new bride that he, too, was aware of her beauty.

"So," Aunt Mavis began, "what brings you two down our way? Just out for a drive?"

"No, not really," Chuck answered. "I had a meeting this afternoon with some other pastors down in Los Angeles, so I brought Jenny with me and we went out to dinner afterward. That's when we decided to stop by here on our way home. We tried to call just before we left, but no one answered."

"We were going to go on without stopping," Jennifer explained, "but then we remembered you were probably just out for your evening walk, so we came by anyway."

"I'm so glad you did, darling," Rachel said. "And you're right. We were out for our evening walk."

"That's right," Aunt Mavis chimed in. "And your mother is getting to be quite a walker, I might add. Why, before you know it, she'll be able to keep up with me."

They all laughed, and Snuffy barked and thumped his tail. "Yes, Snuf," Aunt Mavis added. "You're getting to be a good walker, too, aren't you, boy?"

"You know, Mom," Chuck said, turning to look at Rachel, "I'll bet all that walking is the reason you're looking so slim and trim these days. I noticed when I came in that you've lost some weight."

Rachel blushed. "Well, yes, I have—about seven or eight pounds—but I didn't realize it showed."

"You bet it does, Mom!" Jennifer exclaimed. "In fact,

everytime we come by here, you look younger and younger. First that new haircut a couple of weeks ago, and now your new figure—I think it's great."

"Well, after all, she's a working woman now," Aunt Mavis smiled. "She has an image to uphold, you know."

Chuck grinned. "Still liking your new job, Mom?"

"I love it, Chuck," Rachel answered. "I really do. Those kids are so special. I never dreamed I'd enjoy working so much. Of course, it's only two mornings a week right now, but I've decided to sign up for some courses next semester and start working toward getting my teaching credentials. I found out I can get all the credits to teach preschool that I need right up here at the college. Isn't that exciting?"

Jennifer jumped up and hurried over to her mother, hugging her tightly. "Oh, Mom, that's great news. I'm so happy for you."

Chuck put his arm around Rachel's shoulders, as Aunt Mavis looked on, beaming. "So, tell us about your job, Mom," Chuck said, as Jennifer squeezed in between him and Aunt Mavis. "What is it you like so much?"

"Well," Rachel began, "there's really not anything I don't like, I suppose. It's a small school with six teachers and four aides. And, of course, you know Joan Mitchell is the director there. It's such a pleasant group, such a nice atmosphere. Susan Frost, the teacher I work with most of the time, is so good with the kids. I've learned a lot just watching her." Rachel looked at her daughter. "When she smiles, she reminds me of you."

Chuck whistled. "She must be a knockout!"

Jennifer smiled and laid her hand on her husband's knee.

"But the children," Rachel went on enthusiastically, "they're the ones I can't wait to see in the mornings. They're precious, just precious! Especially Jeremy. Oh, I know I shouldn't have favorites, but Jeremy is so sweet. Just this morning he told me he wished he could have me for a grandma." She stopped, glancing at Chuck and Jennifer to see if either of them had reacted to the word "grandma."

Jennifer's cheeks flushed a deep red, and she looked at Chuck. He raised his eyebrows at her questioningly.

"Um, actually, Mom—" She turned around. "—And Aunt Mavis—there is something Chuck and I want to tell you." She got up from the couch and knelt down on the floor at her mother's feet. She took Rachel's hands, then glanced up at Chuck once more. He nodded.

"Mom," Jennifer went on, looking into Rachel's eyes, "you're going to be a grandmother. In early May." She paused. "What do you think of that?"

Rachel didn't answer. She didn't even try to stop the tears as they welled up in her eyes and spilled over onto her cheeks.

Chuck tightened his arm around Rachel's shoulders. "Are you okay, Mom?"

Rachel nodded, trying to think of the right things to say. She mustn't let them know this was not a surprise.

Jennifer was frowning again, as she always did when she was worried or upset. "Mom?"

"I'm fine," Rachel managed to answer finally. "I'm just so very happy, that's all."

Jennifer's frown disappeared, and her smile lit up her entire face. "Oh, Mom, I'm so glad!"

"Well, congratulations!" Aunt Mavis cried, jumping up and clapping her hands together. "This is the best news I've heard since I can't remember when. This calls for a celebration! I'll go put the teakettle on."

"Sounds great," Chuck agreed. "I'll help you."

As Chuck and Aunt Mavis went off into the kitchen, Jennifer sat down next to her mother. "Oh, Mom, I'm sorry we didn't tell you sooner. I just didn't want to upset you."

Rachel looked at her daughter. "What did I ever do to deserve you?" she asked, wiping a tear from her cheek.

Jennifer hugged her. "Oh, Mom, I love you so much. If we have a girl, we're going to name her Rachel, after her wonderful grandmother."

Rachel swallowed hard and smiled. She was afraid to ask if they'd decided on a boy's name.

* * *

Rachel climbed into bed, exhausted. She wondered if Chuck and Jennifer had gotten home yet. They'll make wonderful parents, she thought. Jenny has always loved children. And Chuck is so gentle and patient. Oh, God, thank you that my daughter has such a happy marriage. Thank you for that at least! She closed her eyes, as images of Chuck and Jennifer floated through her mind. Suddenly, they were walking down the aisle at church, Jennifer in her long, flowing wedding gown, Chuck in his tuxedo. Rachel looked around. Where was everyone? Why hadn't their friends come to the wedding? She was the only one in the church besides Chuck and Jennifer.

And then she realized why no one was there. They were in the wrong church! How had they gotten here? All the guests must be waiting for them at another church! Rachel felt so stupid. She knew it must be her fault that Chuck and Jennifer had come to the wrong church with her. I must stop them, she thought. There's not even a minister here to marry them. She opened her mouth. "Wait!" she wanted to cry, but nothing came out. She tried to run to them, but her legs moved so slowly, and Chuck and Jennifer were getting farther and farther away from her.

What was that noise? Was it a choir? Was someone there, after all? Who's singing? Stop that singing! This is the wrong wedding!

The noise was growing louder now, and Rachel put her hands over her ears. But as the sound got closer, she realized it wasn't a choir she was hearing—it was a baby crying.

She dragged her legs, trying to run and warn them. She must stop the wedding. Why wouldn't anyone help? Jenny! Chuck! Stop!

"I'll help you, Rachel."

Rachel froze. She felt a hand on her shoulder. Horrified, she turned. She couldn't see his face, but she knew who he was.

Oh, dear God, why can't I scream? She could hear the organ now. Rachel looked back toward the front of the church to see who was playing it. The only people she could see were the bride and groom, kneeling. Why were they kneeling? There was no one there to bless them.

The couple got up and turned around, as if to walk back down the aisle. That's when Rachel saw the baby in Jennifer's arms. The baby was still crying. Jennifer looked so happy. Didn't she understand?

The hand on Rachel's shoulder moved slowly across her back and up her neck. She gasped as she felt her long hair being unpinned from the back of her neck and falling down onto her shoulders. He stroked her hair, then lifted it gently as he kissed her neck, her shoulder.

Rachel closed her eyes and leaned against him. His breath was warm against her skin, and the smell of leather and Old Spice after-shave made her weak. His other arm was around her waist. Then she heard the baby again.

Her eyes snapped open and she was suddenly aware that she was standing in church in her nightgown. Oh, God, how could I? Here in church—and in front of the baby! She pushed the man away from her, wishing she could get home and take a shower before the wedding started.

"I want a divorce, Rachel."

Rachel's eyes grew wide. She looked behind her. The man was gone.

"I want a divorce, Rachel."

She could hear her heart pounding now, and she was having trouble breathing.

"Daddy, don't leave!" It was Jennifer. "Don't leave us, Daddy!"

Then she saw him. He was standing in front of Chuck and Jennifer, looking exactly as he had when Rachel had first met him twenty-seven years earlier. The muscles in his shoulders and arms rippled under his white T-shirt.

"What are you doing with my baby?" Bill was asking Jennifer, his arms reaching toward her. "Give me my baby."

Jennifer was crying. "No, Daddy, no! You can't have him. He's mine."

Chuck, help us! Rachel thought, but Chuck just stood by, watching.

Suddenly, Bill was running down the aisle with the baby in his arms. Jennifer was screaming. "No, no! Daddy, come back." Then she spun around and looked at Rachel. "Help me, Mommy! Please!"

As Jennifer fell into her mother's arms, Rachel heard herself say, "Don't worry, darling. We'll get a lawyer. He'll know what to do. I promise. We'll get our baby back, you'll see. Everything's going to be all right."

"And just what is going on here?"

Rachel and Jennifer looked up to see Aunt Mavis, hands on hips, standing in the middle of the aisle.

"All your guests are waiting up in the balcony to give you your presents," Aunt Mavis informed Jennifer. "We've been waiting and waiting. Come along, my dear. There'll be plenty of time for tears later."

Rachel and Jennifer followed Aunt Mavis up the stairs to the balcony. Chuck was already there, sitting in a sandbox full of brightly wrapped packages, playing with a small towheaded boy.

The little boy looked up and grinned. "Hi, Grandma."

Rachel's hand flew to her mouth. Jeremy! What was he doing here?

Jeremy jumped up. "Want to see what I can do, Grandma?" He ran to the edge of the balcony and climbed up on the railing. "I can do tricks."

"No, Jeremy, no! Get down!" Rachel shrieked.

But it was too late. Rachel caught only a flicker of fear in the trusting brown eyes before the blond head disappeared over the other side of the railing.

Chapter 6

"Are you sure you'll be all right, my dear? I can change my plans and do my shopping another day if you'd like me to stay with you."

Rachel was lying on the couch in the den with a cool cloth over her eyes. "No, Aunt Mavis. I'll be fine, really. I've just got a slight headache from not sleeping too well last night. I've taken two aspirin, and if I just lie here quietly for a while I'm sure I'll feel much better. You go on, please."

Aunt Mavis hesitated. "Well . . . if you're sure."

Rachel lifted the cloth from her eyes and looked up at her aunt. "I'm sure, Aunt Mavis."

"All right then. I'll see you before lunch." Aunt Mavis turned to leave, then stopped. "Can I bring you anything, my dear?"

Rachel covered her eyes once more. "No, Aunt Mavis. Nothing. I just want to sleep."

She sighed with relief when she heard Aunt Mavis close the front door behind her. After her nightmare, she had been too confused and too terrified to go back to sleep. Although she had told herself over and over again that it was only a dream, she couldn't shake the feeling of dread that had settled over her. Aunt Mavis's nonstop chatter all morning had grated on Rachel's nerves so badly she had retreated to the den in an effort to find some peace and quiet. When Aunt Mavis had announced her plans to go shopping, Rachel had breathed a prayer of thanks.

She was just drifting off to sleep when the doorbell brought her back. *Now who can that be? Maybe Aunt Mavis has forgotten her key again, although I certainly didn't expect her back so soon.*

She dragged herself up from the couch and laid the cloth down on the coffee table. Pulling on her faded robe, she slid into her slippers and shuffled down the hall toward the front door, wishing she'd taken the time to put on some makeup or at least combed her hair. She opened the door, then froze.

Bill stood on the doorstep, freshly groomed in his three-piece suit, with papers clenched in his hand. Without waiting for Rachel to say anything, he stepped inside the house, slamming the door behind him. He lifted the papers he was holding and shook them in Rachel's face.

"I just had these divorce papers handed to me this morning, Rachel," he growled. "Just what do you think you're trying to do? What do you want from me—blood?"

Rachel opened her mouth, but all she could think of was how naked and ashamed she had felt in her dream the night before when she had realized she was standing in church in her nightgown. She pulled her robe around her and knotted the belt tightly, as the familiar twitch began over her right eye.

Bill slapped the papers against the palm of his free hand. Rachel flinched.

"Talk to me, Rachel. I want some answers, and I want them now."

"I need to sit down," Rachel said weakly, turning and walking toward the den. She sank down onto the couch where she'd been earlier, and stared into the fireplace at last night's ashes.

Bill had followed her to the den door. "I don't know what you're trying to pull, Rachel, but it's not going to work." He strode to the easy chair across from the couch and sat down. "Look at me, Rachel," he ordered.

Slowly, Rachel raised her head and looked at the man she had loved for so many years. She hated him now for what he had done to her; she hated herself for the tears welling up inside her.

Vaguely, she became aware of Snuffy, scratching and whining at the sliding glass door, wanting to come in, but she ignored him. "I told you I have nothing more to say to you, Bill," she said softly.

"That's why I had the rest of your things sent to you. I don't want to see you."

"The rest of my things!" Bill exploded, jumping up. "You call three boxes of clothes and some personal items from my desk 'the rest of my things'? I worked hard for all of this! If you think I'm going to walk away and give it all to you, you're crazy! How do you expect me to live?"

Rachel's eyes widened and she lifted her head higher. The threat of tears was gone. "The last I heard you were doing just fine living in Sheryl's apartment. What's the matter? Isn't it big enough for a nursery?"

"Leave Sheryl out of this, Rachel. This is between you and me."

Rachel almost laughed. "Is that right? Funny. I don't recall being the one to bring Sheryl into this in the first place." She smiled. "Besides, you pay her a good salary for being your . . . secretary, don't you? Why don't you just live on that? Or is she planning to quit so she can stay home and take care of your new baby?"

"Shut up, Rachel!" Bill bellowed. His face was red now, and his jaw muscles twitched as he stared down at her.

"Oh, I'm sorry," Rachel apologized. "I guess I misunderstood. I thought you wanted me to talk to you."

"What in the world is going on in here?"

Rachel jumped, startled at the sight of Jennifer standing in the doorway, staring at them.

"Daddy, what are you doing here? I could hear you all the way out at the front door."

Bill's face paled and he seemed to shrink, but he didn't answer.

Jennifer hurried to Rachel. "Are you all right, Mom?"

"I'm fine, darling," Rachel assured her. "Sit down, honey, please. Don't let yourself get upset."

Jennifer sat down next to her mother. Bill was standing in front of the fireplace, clutching the divorce papers.

"I'd better go," he said finally.

"No, Daddy. Please stay. We need to talk."

Bill swallowed hard. "I can't, Jenny. I know I've been avoiding you, but there are some things I just can't discuss with you, baby."

Jennifer got up and walked over to Bill. "Daddy, I'm not a baby anymore. I'm a grown woman." She paused. "I'm going to have a baby of my own."

Bill looked into his daughter's eyes. "Oh, Jenny, I didn't know."

"I wanted to tell you, Dad, but . . . ."

Suddenly they were in each other's arms. Rachel wanted to scream at Jennifer to get away, to run! Don't let him hold you, Jenny! Don't let him touch you! But she just sat there silently, feeling like an intruder.

Jennifer pushed herself back and looked up at Bill. "Please sit down and talk to us, Daddy. Please?"

Bill looked at his daughter for a moment, and then nodded. He went back to the easy chair and sat down stiffly. Jennifer sat back down beside Rachel.

The silence was heavy, uncomfortable. "I shouldn't be here," Rachel said. "I'll just leave you two alone."

Jennifer put her hand on her mother's arm. "No, Mom. Stay, please."

Bill cleared his throat, but no one seemed willing to begin.

"All right," Jennifer said softly. "I'll start this thing. Daddy?"

Bill looked at Jennifer.

"Daddy, why did you leave Mom?"

Bill's cheeks colored. "Jenny, you already know the reasons."

"I want to hear you say it, Daddy. Don't you think it's time for some honesty around here?"

Bill continued to look at his daughter, the pain on his face making him appear years older than he was. He sighed deeply. "All right, Jennifer. I left your mother because . . . I'm in love with someone else."

"And?"

Bill's eyes were pleading, but Jennifer didn't back down.

Don't say it! Rachel begged silently. Oh, God, don't let him say it!

"And she's going to have my baby," Bill mumbled, dropping his gaze.

Rachel's hand flew to her mouth, but she said nothing. All the pain of the past weeks seemed to pour in on her like a tidal wave. Everything she had built her life around for years, all her dreams, even her faith, had come crashing down around her. What next, God? What next?

"Are you going to marry her, Dad?"

The twitch over Rachel's eye had grown worse and she was gasping for air. There was a bitter taste rising up at the bottom of her throat. She jumped up from the couch and ran blindly for the bathroom. She heard voices behind her, but she locked the door and fell to her knees beside the toilet, coughing and heaving into the bowl. When she was through, she flushed the toilet and leaned her head against the cool porcelain, as hot tears dripped off her nose and cheeks into the water below.

"Mom! Open the door, please. Mom! Let me in!"

"Oh, God, make them go away," Rachel moaned.

The banging on the door made her jump. "Rachel!" It was Bill. "Rachel, you open this door right now, or I'll break it down. Do you hear me, Rachel?"

Rachel stood up slowly and walked to the sink. Turning on the cold water, she splashed her face, then unlocked the door. It flew open as Bill and Jennifer burst in. They stopped, staring at Rachel as she patted her face dry with a towel.

Setting the towel down, she looked at Bill. "What's the matter, Bill?" she asked flatly. "Are you disappointed? Did you think I came in here to kill myself?"

She turned to Jennifer. "I'm all right now, Jenny. I'm sorry if I frightened you. I'm just not feeling too well, I'm afraid. I didn't sleep much last night."

Rachel walked past them into the den. She picked up the cloth she had been using earlier and placed it over her eyes as she sat back down on the couch.

"Mom?" Jennifer was kneeling beside her mother, as Bill looked on. "Mom, I'm sorry. I didn't mean to upset you."

Rachel removed the cloth and smiled at her daughter. "It's all right, darling. It wasn't your fault."

Bill flushed again. "I'd better leave now."

"Oh, please don't." Rachel continued. "Really, I'd love to hear about your plans. Will it be a big wedding?"

Bill turned and walked out of the room.

"Daddy, wait," Jennifer cried. She looked at Rachel, who had put the cloth back over her eyes, then jumped up and ran after her father. "Daddy!"

They stopped outside the den door, and Rachel listened from underneath her damp cloth.

"Jenny, I'm sorry, but I've got to go. I'm only making things worse by staying."

"But, Daddy, why did you come? Were you going to try to talk things over with Mom? Work things out?"

For a moment, neither of them spoke. Finally, Bill answered. "No, baby. I didn't come to work things out with your mother. That's over, Jenny. You must realize that, don't you? There's no going back. Our marriage died years ago; we just never bothered to bury it. Somehow I thought we could go on living that way—with no love between us, nothing in common—but then I met Sheryl. We never intended to fall in love, Jenny. But things happen. Can't you understand that? At first, it was just lunch or long talks when things were slow at the office, but one day I realized I wanted more than that. Sheryl made me feel alive, Jenny. She made me feel important. She cared about what I had to say. She cared about me. Oh, baby, I'm sorry that my happiness has caused you so much pain, but Sheryl's given me the love that I've needed for so long."

"That's not fair!" Jennifer cried. "That's just not fair! Mom loves you. I know she does. Dad, she's been your wife for twenty-five years. Doesn't that mean anything to you?"

Bill's voice was so low now that Rachel had to strain to hear his answer. "Of course it means something to me, Jenny. But—"

"But what?" Jennifer was crying. "She wasn't young enough or sexy enough for you anymore? Is that it? Dad, you're forty-eight years old. Sheryl's not much older than I am."

"Is it her age that bothers you, Jenny? Would all this bother you less if I'd left your mother for someone my own age? Or older? What difference does age make? I love Sheryl, and she loves me. We're happy together, Jenny. Can't you try to be just a little bit glad for me that I've finally found some happiness in my life?"

"But what about Mom's happiness?" Jennifer screamed. "And mine? Do you care about that at all? Do you care about anyone's happiness besides your own?"

"Now you're the one who's not being fair, Jenny. Of course I care about your happiness—and your mother's. But sometimes we have to make choices."

"Oh, I see. You care about us, but not as much as you care about Sheryl and your new child. You just trade your old family in on a new one when the old one gets a little worn out, is that it?"

"Baby, please! Listen to me, Jenny. No one could ever take your place. Don't you know that? Of course I'll love my new child when it's born, but that doesn't mean I'll love you any less!"

"Oh, Daddy!"

Rachel wondered if Bill was holding Jennifer again. When Jennifer was little, it had always been Bill she had run to when she was hurt.

"Jenny," Bill was saying. "I'm glad for you—about the baby, I mean. How long have you known?"

"Since right before you—" She stopped. "For a few weeks. The baby's due in early May." Bill didn't respond.

"When's your . . . when's your baby due?" Jennifer asked.

"In May."

They were silent again. Rachel wondered if she should go check on Jennifer.

"Well, I'd better go, Jenny."

"Oh, Daddy, please don't!"

"I have to, baby."

"When will I see you?"

"Would you like to come to our apartment for dinner sometime? You and Chuck?"

Rachel could almost see Jennifer stiffen.

"No! I will not have dinner with you at your . . . apartment! I want to see you, Daddy, but I never want to see that woman—or her child."

"Oh, Jenny, please, listen to me. Baby, we can't go through the rest of our lives like this. You're my daughter. I love you. But I love Sheryl, too. Don't you think you could at least try to be friends with her? For my sake?"

"I will never be friends with her. And I will never visit with you when you're together. I'm sorry, Daddy, but that's the way it is."

Bill sighed loudly. "All right. If that's the way you want it. I'll call you, okay?"

Jennifer didn't answer, and in a moment Rachel heard the front door close.

"Daddy, wait. Come back. We're your family. Can't you see that? Daddy, don't leave us!"

A chill crawled up Rachel's spine as she remembered Jennifer standing in church in her wedding dress, her arms outstretched, as Bill ran down the aisle carrying the baby.

Suddenly, Rachel heard a moan, and then a thud. She ran into the hallway and gasped, as she saw her daughter doubled up on the floor, clutching her stomach.

"Mama," Jennifer whispered. "Mama, help me! The baby. . . ."

"Oh, my God!" Rachel couldn't move. She stood there, staring at her daughter, as the memory of her dream and Jeremy's trusting brown eyes flashed through her mind.

"Help me, Mama!"

Rachel shook her head, trying to think clearly, then raced to the kitchen phone. Her hands were shaking so badly she could hardly dial. "Dear God, what's the doctor's number? I can't remember!"

She grabbed the phone book, flipping the pages frantically. It slipped from her trembling hands and fell to the floor.

"Oh, God!" she cried, putting her hands over her face. "Help me!" The operator, she thought. She'll know what to do. She grabbed the phone and punched "O."

"We need an ambulance!" she cried when she heard the operator's voice. "Please help us!"

"Yes, ma'am. Calm down now. Where are you calling from?"

"I'm at . . . 12789 Sunset Terrace. Please hurry!"

The phone was ringing again. Oh, hurry, hurry!

"Emergency. May I help you?"

"We need an ambulance! And please hurry!"

"All right, ma'am. Now, where are you calling from?"

"We're at 12789 Sunset Terrace. It's my daughter! Please help us!"

"Calm down, ma'am. Can you tell me your name and what's wrong with your daughter, please?"

Rachel took a deep breath. "Yes, all right. My name is Rachel Webster. My daughter is pregnant. I . . . think she's having a miscarriage."

"All right. We'll be there as quickly as possible. Meanwhile, just keep her calm. Is she lying down?"

"She's on the floor."

"Is she conscious?"

"Yes! Yes, she's conscious! Please, no more questions! Just send help!"

She slammed the receiver down and hurried back to her daughter. Kneeling beside her, she took Jennifer's hand. "Are you all right, darling?"

Jennifer opened her eyes. "I'm okay, Mom. But it hurts. And I'm so cold!"

"I'll be right back, honey."

Rachel ran to the linen closet and grabbed a blanket. She laid it gently over Jennifer. "Would you like a pillow?"

Jennifer shook her head weakly. Rachel brushed Jennifer's hair back from her forehead. Her hair was damp, forming ringlets around her ashen face. "I think I'm bleeding, Mama," she whispered. Dear God, where's that ambulance?

Jennifer moaned again. "My baby. Am I going to lose my baby?"

"Of course not, Jenny. Everything's going to be just fine, darling. Please don't worry." This is all your fault, Bill Webster. If only you hadn't come over here . . . .

"Mama. Mama, please call Chuck. I want him with me."

Rachel bent and kissed her daughter on the forehead. "I'll call him right now, sweetheart. You just lie here quietly. I'll be right back."

This time she dialed the phone quickly.

"Good morning. Grace Church."

"Pastor Miller, please. This is his mother-in-law." Dear God, how do I tell him?

"Hi, Mom! Are you and Jenny having a nice visit? She just decided at the last minute to drive down and—"

"Chuck," Rachel interrupted, "it's the baby. You'd better come right away. We're waiting for the ambulance."

"I'm on my way."

Rachel hung up the phone just as Aunt Mavis walked in the front door. "I'm home!" she called cheerily. She walked toward the den, but stopped when she saw Jennifer lying on the floor.

"Thank God, you're home!" Rachel exclaimed, coming up behind her. "Can you stay with Jenny for a minute while I throw on some clothes? I want to ride in the ambulance with her."

Aunt Mavis dropped to her knees beside Jennifer. Then she looked up at Rachel. "The baby?"

Rachel nodded, as the scream of an approaching siren reached their ears.

Chapter 7

The ride in the ambulance had seemed interminable. Rachel had tried to encourage Jennifer, assuring her that everything would be fine once they arrived at the hospital. But now she sat in the waiting room next to Aunt Mavis, unable to convince herself there was any hope that her grandchild might survive. She knew Aunt Mavis was praying. She wanted to scream at her, "Why bother? Don't you realize he doesn't care?"

She buried her head in her hands. Oh, God, why Jenny? Why punish Jenny? Her mind went back to the morning she had lain in this very hospital twenty-two years earlier, while Bill paced anxiously in the waiting room. It had been a difficult pregnancy, and there were times she had thought she might lose her baby. But Jennifer had been born healthy and strong, and Rachel had thought her life was complete.

Then, two years later, she had become pregnant again. They had been overjoyed, hoping this time for a son. But Rachel had lost the baby in her third month. They had tried twice more over the next five years, but Jennifer was to be an only child.

That's when they had moved to their new home, and Rachel had abandoned all hope of ever having another baby. She resigned herself to living in a house she hated with a man who was seldom home, and had dedicated herself to being as perfect a mother as she possibly could be to Jennifer.

"Mom? Aunt Mavis?"

Rachel jerked her head up and saw Chuck. Aunt Mavis had already gotten up and was putting her arms around him.

"Oh, my dear, we're so glad you're here."

Chuck hugged Aunt Mavis, then looked from her to Rachel. "How's Jenny? Can I see her?"

Rachel shook her head slowly. "We haven't heard a thing."

Chuck and Aunt Mavis sat down on either side of Rachel, and Chuck took Rachel's hand. "Mom, what happened?"

Rachel's eyes filled with tears. "Oh, Chuck!" She took a deep breath. "I'm afraid Jenny arrived while Bill was there. We were having a terrible argument, and she became so upset." She collapsed on Chuck's shoulder, sobbing. "Oh, Chuck, I'm so sorry."

Chuck held her gently until her sobs had quieted. Then he asked, "If Dad was there when all this happened, where is he now? Why isn't he here?"

Rachel drew back and shook her head again. "He wasn't there. It happened right after he walked out the door. Poor Jenny! She begged him not to leave."

"Did the doctors say anything when you brought her in?" Chuck asked. "Anything at all?"

"Nothing," Rachel answered, choking back another sob. "We've just been sitting here, waiting."

Chuck stood up. "I'm going to go see what I can find out."

"Would you like me to come with you, dear?" Aunt Mavis asked.

Chuck shook his head, his lips pressed tightly together. "I'll only be a minute."

Rachel watched him walk out of the room. She knew he was as scared as she was.

Aunt Mavis put her hand on Rachel's arm. "You didn't tell me about Bill."

Rachel shrugged. "There's nothing to tell. He came over ranting and raving about the divorce papers I had served on him. Not that he's so upset about the divorce. After all, he's the one who wanted it. It's just that he doesn't like the financial settlement I've asked for."

Aunt Mavis raised her eyebrows. "I didn't even realize you had filed for divorce. You didn't tell me about that, either."

"I wasn't aware that I had to tell you everything, Aunt Mavis!" Rachel answered defensively. "Besides, what else did you expect me to do, under the circumstances?"

"Well . . . I had hoped you might wait awhile before doing anything so . . . rash. Are you sure this is what you want?"

Rachel's eyes opened wide. "What I want? What do you mean, what I want? I don't remember being consulted about any of this. My life has been decided for me by an unfaithful husband and his cheap tramp of a secretary. I'm only doing what I have to do, Aunt Mavis. I would hardly consider this a rash decision. In fact, it's probably the first wise decision I've made in years. And if he thinks I'm going to back down on even one point in my demands, he's wrong. He told Jenny he had to make a choice. Well, he's made it, and as far as I'm concerned, he's going to live with it."

Just then a young doctor in a green smock walked in. "Mrs. Webster?"

Rachel jumped up. "I'm Rachel Webster."

Aunt Mavis stood up and put her arm around Rachel's waist.

The doctor stuck out his hand. "I'm Dr. Hunter."

When Rachel didn't respond, Aunt Mavis shook the doctor's hand. "I'm Mavis Whittaker, Rachel's aunt."

Rachel didn't notice Dr. Hunter's sandy brown hair or his haggard appearance. She only saw his eyes. And she knew.

"Can we sit down?" the doctor asked softly.

Chuck walked in just as they sat down. He hurried over to them. "Are you Jenny's doctor?"

Dr. Hunter stood up again and shook Chuck's hand. "I'm Dr. Hunter. You must be Jennifer's husband."

Chuck nodded. "How is she?"

The doctor indicated a chair to Chuck, and they both sat down. "Jennifer's going to be all right." He looked around at each one of them. "But I'm afraid she's lost the baby."

Chuck buried his head in his hands and groaned. Aunt Mavis gasped and tears filled her eyes. Rachel said nothing. She stood up and walked silently across the room, stopping and staring out the window. She was amazed to see cars driving by, people coming and going as if nothing had changed.

She heard voices behind her—Chuck, Aunt Mavis, the young doctor with the sad eyes—but she didn't care what they were saying. The baby was dead. What else was there to say?

She lost track of how long she'd been standing there, staring out the window, until Aunt Mavis came over and put her hand on Rachel's shoulder. She turned slowly toward her aunt.

"Chuck's gone in to see Jenny for a few minutes," Aunt Mavis explained. "The doctor said we shouldn't tire her right now, but we can see her this evening. Shall we go on home, my dear? Chuck will call us if there's any change."

Rachel nodded. She went back to the chair where she had been sitting and picked up her purse. As they walked out the door and started down the long corridor, she froze. There, at the nurses' station, stood Bill—and Sheryl.

"I'm Bill Webster," Bill was explaining to the nurse. "I'm Jennifer Miller's father. I just had a call from her husband that she was here. Is she all right?"

Before the nurse could answer, Rachel walked up behind them. "Jenny is fine," she said coldly, "considering you just murdered her baby!"

Bill and Sheryl turned. Their faces were pale, and Rachel was surprised to see tears in Sheryl's eyes.

"What did you say?" Bill asked, his eyes wild with fear.

"Jenny's baby is dead." She spoke slowly, deliberately, wanting each word to cut as deeply as possible. "And it's your fault."

She turned sharply and walked down the hall, her head high. Aunt Mavis looked helplessly at Bill, then hurried down the hallway after Rachel.

* * *

It had been a long and painful weekend. Rachel and Aunt Mavis had gone with Chuck on Monday to bring Jennifer home.

They hadn't wanted to leave that evening to drive back to Ventura, but Jennifer had insisted that she and Chuck needed some time alone.

And now it was Tuesday morning and Rachel had just pulled up in front of the preschool. Thank God I have my job to keep me busy, she thought. I couldn't bear sitting home with Aunt Mavis today.

Joan looked surprised when Rachel walked in. "Good morning," she smiled. "I didn't think you'd be in today. You know we can cover for you if you want to spend some more time with Jenny."

Rachel shook her head. "Jenny's all right. I need to be here, Joan."

Joan nodded and walked over to Rachel, hugging her briefly. "Please let me know if there's anything I can do, Rachel."

Rachel didn't answer.

"Some of the children have already arrived," Joan went on. "They're out on the playground with Susan."

Although the morning sun shone brightly, Rachel left her sweater on as she walked out onto the playground. She could hardly believe it was November already. It was so hard to keep track of time lately. The last few weeks seemed to blur into one long nightmare.

Susan was supervising the sandbox when Rachel walked up. "Well, look who's here!" Susan announced.

Several children stopped playing and peered up at her.

"Hi, Miss Rachel."

"Hi, Miss Rachel."

Jeremy's blond hair glistened in the sun, and his brown eyes danced as he grinned in recognition. "Miss Rachel!" he cried, jumping up from his pile of sand.

Rachel almost fell over as Jeremy threw his arms around her legs.

Jeremy looked up at her adoringly. "Miss Rachel, will you push me on the swing?"

72

Rachel took a deep breath and nodded, steeling herself against the tears that were welling up inside her. "Of course I will," she answered carefully.

Jeremy took her hand and led her to the swings. The lump in her throat was growing, and she knew she wasn't going to make it. The tears reached her eyes, and she quickly grabbed a tissue from her apron pocket.

"Are you crying, Miss Rachel?"

Rachel shook her head. "No, Jeremy, I . . . I just have something in my eye."

His little face drew up in a frown. "Do you want me to fix it? I can get it out for you."

Rachel knelt down beside him. "I'll bet you can," she said softly, handing him the tissue.

He worked carefully and gently, his face serious and intense. "How's that?"

She blinked. "You know, Jeremy, I think you got it."

He grinned. "I knew I could do it."

"I knew you could too, Jeremy."

Suddenly Jeremy's arms were around her neck. "You're the best teacher in the whole world, Miss Rachel! I still wish I could have you for a grandma."

* * *

As Rachel left work and climbed into her car shortly after noon that day, she decided she wasn't ready to go home just yet. Turning the car toward the beach, she tried to block out the events of the last few days. She had thought, after Bill left her for Sheryl, that nothing worse could possibly happen in her life. She had been wrong. Watching her daughter suffer the loss of her baby had been almost more than Rachel could bear.

Turning left just past the railroad tracks, she began to follow the familiar two-lane road that ran parallel with the southern California coastline. So much has changed, she thought sadly, driving past the new high-rise hotels, restaurants, and condominiums. I hardly recognize Ventura anymore!

She sighed, remembering how it had been in the late fifties when she had come here so often as a teenager with her girl-friends. And how Jenny had loved playing here when she was lit-tle! She had been frightened of the water, but she would sit contentedly beside her mother for hours, patiently digging in the sand, chattering away while Rachel dozed in the sun.

Rachel pulled into the parking lot beside the pier and stopped. She rolled down her window to let in the cool ocean breeze. She shivered slightly, enjoying the fresh salty air.

The beach was deserted except for a few scattered seagulls, diving and swooping over the water. Two lone fishermen stood on the pier, their poles hanging over the edge. Rachel wondered what they were thinking as they gazed at the sea below them. She watched them for some time, but they never seemed to speak to each other.

Rachel closed her eyes. It seemed such a few years ago that she and Bill had run, laughing, along this same beach. How many times had Bill chased her out to the end of that very pier, threatening to throw her off the end and make her swim to shore if she wouldn't agree to marry him? She had giggled and squealed as they ran, knowing all along that he would never throw her off the pier, and knowing also that there was nothing she wanted more in all the world than to marry Bill Webster.

What am I doing? she thought, sitting up straight and shaking her head. I don't need this! She started the car and backed out of her parking space, deciding suddenly to go by her lawyer's office and see if he had a moment to see her. She wanted to tell him about Bill's reaction to the divorce papers.

There was no one in the waiting room when Rachel walked into the office. Almost immediately after she closed the front door, the sliding glass window opened and Sylvia poked her head out.

"Well, hello, Mrs. Webster! How are you?"

Rachel was pleased that Sylvia remembered her. "I'm fine,

thank you, Sylvia," she said with a smile. "I'm afraid I don't have an appointment, but I just wondered if maybe . . . well, do you suppose Mr. Langsford could work me into his schedule some-time this afternoon? I only need to see him for a few minutes."

Sylvia glanced at her watch. "He usually goes to lunch at twelve-thirty, but if you'll hang on, I'll see what we can work out. He's with a client now, but I'm sure he's almost finished. Would you like some coffee while you're waiting?"

Rachel thought of her last visit to the office when the red-haired woman had come in. "Coffee would be nice," she answered. "Just a little sugar, please."

Sylvia turned to the coffee pot behind her and filled a cup with coffee, dropping in a sugar cube. She added a stirrer and handed it to Rachel.

"Thanks." Rachel smiled again, then walked over to the couch and sat down in front of the table with the magazines. She stirred her coffee, then sipped it carefully. It tasted as if it had been sitting for hours, but at least it was hot.

As she flipped through a fashion magazine, the door to the inner offices opened and a heavyset woman with glasses stepped out. "Thanks again, Mr. Langsford. I'll talk to you soon."

"Good-bye, Mrs. Brownley," Mr. Langsford answered, step-ping into the waiting room. "And don't worry about a thing."

The woman walked out of the office, and Mr. Langsford looked down at Rachel. "Well, Mrs. Webster," he smiled, "Sylvia told me you were here. So good to see you again. Come on in."

Rachel stood up hesitantly. "Are you sure? I mean, Sylvia said you usually go to lunch about now. I can come back later."

"Nonsense." He patted his slight paunch. "It won't hurt me to put off lunch for a little while." He turned to hold the door open for Rachel, then stopped. "Wait a minute. Have you had lunch?"

Rachel flushed. "Well, no, but, I, uh. . . ."

Mr. Langsford's grin seemed to spread across his entire face. "Wonderful! Let's have a working lunch! What do you say? Come on, it's on me."

When Rachel still hesitated, he winked. "Besides, I can write it off."

Rachel smiled back in spite of herself. She nodded. "All right, sure. I was feeling a little bit hungry."

"Sylvia, I'll be back in time for my two o'clock appointment."

"Have a nice lunch." Sylvia called after them.

"Where would you like to go?" he asked, as they stood in front of the elevator.

"Oh, I don't know. Anything's fine, really."

"I know a great little deli, just down the street. In fact, it's so close we can walk."

Rachel nodded. "That would be fine, thank you, Mr. Langsford."

The elevator door slid open. "Cal. Please, call me Cal. And may I call you Rachel?"

Rachel nodded again, flustered. "Of course, Mr.—I mean, Cal."

Rachel was self-conscious as they walked down the street. She stared straight ahead, trying desperately to think of something to say.

"A penny for your thoughts," Cal said finally.

Rachel looked up at him. "I'll tell you," she said smiling slightly, "but I'll bet you'll charge me a lot more than a penny."

Cal threw his head back and laughed. "I knew there was a sense of humor under there somewhere."

He opened the door to the deli, and Rachel walked in ahead of him. He took her arm and steered her to a table. "How's this?"

"Fine, thank you."

"So," Cal began, after the waitress had taken their orders, "what can I help you with, Rachel?"

Rachel twisted her napkin nervously. "I . . . well, I just wanted to let you know that Bill got the papers, and . . . well, he's pretty angry. In fact, he's furious. I think he may fight us."

"Of course he'll fight us," Cal agreed. "I warned you about that when we had the conditions of the settlement drawn up, Rachel."

76

She looked up into his kind, gray eyes. "Rachel, I still think your demands are unreasonable." He held up his hand as she started to protest. "Wait. Listen to me, please. I know I'm your lawyer and you're paying me to represent you, but that also means I have to advise you as to what I think are your best interests. Rachel, I want you to get a fair settlement out of all of this. God knows you deserve it after what he's pulled. But you do have the money your parents left you, which is quite a sizable amount. Not to mention the fact that Bill has agreed to let you have the house and the car—both of which are paid for—and a generous amount of alimony. So it's not as if you were financially destitute. Bill only wants to keep the business for himself. I think any judge will consider that a fair request if Bill decides to fight this. We'd have better chance if you were willing to give a little."

"He killed my grandchild," Rachel stated flatly.

"What?"

Rachel took a deep breath and related the ugly details of the last few days. "And you expect me to be charitable to him?" she finished.

Their lunches came, and neither of them spoke as they munched their sandwiches. Finally, Cal looked up at her. Rachel thought she saw a hint of wetness in his eyes.

"I see it all the time," he said. "Families torn apart, lives destroyed—you'd think I'd be used to it by now." He shook his head. "I know a little bit about how you feel, Rachel. My wife, Edith, left me two years ago. I couldn't believe it. Oh, she didn't leave me for another man; she just said she needed to 'find herself.' Can you imagine? After raising four kids, at forty-nine she decides to find herself." He smiled wryly and shrugged. "I guess she's still looking."

All at once, Rachel was overwhelmed with the realization that men, too, could be hurt. This big strong man sitting across the table from her, poking at his potato salad with a plastic fork, suddenly looked very vulnerable. Impulsively, she reached out and covered his hand with her own.

Chapter 8

"It's clouding up a bit," Aunt Mavis commented, peering up at the half-covered moon. "It'll rain by morning."

Rachel looked up at the sky. "How can you tell? The weatherman said partly cloudy, but he didn't mention anything about rain."

Aunt Mavis shrugged and pulled lightly on Snuffy's leash. "I can tell."

It had seemed so cold when they first stepped out into the mid-November darkness, but after several minutes of brisk walking, Rachel's cheeks had taken on a rosy glow, and her hands had warmed up enough to pull them out of her pockets and swing them at her sides. *Aunt Mavis is so stubborn*, she thought, shaking her head. *I suppose she thinks she knows more than the weathermen.*

"Well," Aunt Mavis said suddenly, "do you want to order the turkey or shall I?"

Rachel frowned. "What?"

"The turkey, my dear. Thanksgiving is less than two weeks away, you know. We'd better start making plans. Jennifer and Chuck will come, of course."

"Yes, I suppose so," Rachel agreed.

"So, what about the turkey? Shall I order it?"

"Why don't you, Aunt Mavis. I don't seem to be feeling very much in the holiday mood these days. I haven't even thought about Christmas."

"Well, you should. It would do you good to get out and do some shopping, maybe even buy yourself some new things. Your clothes are just hanging on you. How much weight have you lost now?"

"Twelve pounds. Do you really think I should buy some new clothes?"

"Why, of course. You don't want to go around looking like a bag lady, for heaven's sake." Aunt Mavis looked over at her niece and grinned. "Besides, don't you want to show off your new figure? What is it they say? If you've got it, flaunt it!"

Rachel's eyes widened and she stopped short. "Aunt Mavis, I can't believe you said that."

Aunt Mavis laughed as she called back over her shoulder, "Come along, my dear, we mustn't break our stride."

Rachel hurried to catch up. "You know, Aunt Mavis, after all these years, you never cease to amaze me."

Aunt Mavis chuckled. "Well, good for me. I'd like to think I still have a few surprises left in me."

They walked on in silence for a few moments until Aunt Mavis said, "You know, Rachel, I've been thinking."

Rachel raised an eyebrow warily, but she didn't answer.

"You seem to be very happy with your new job," Aunt Mavis went on. "And I know you're looking forward to starting those classes next semester. That part of your life seems headed in the right direction, but. . . ."

Her pause made Rachel uneasy.

"I know you don't want to talk about this, Rachel, but don't you ever wonder why? I mean, wouldn't you like to sort through things and get to the root cause of what happened to your marriage?"

Rachel stopped walking again. This time Aunt Mavis stopped, too, while Snuffy tugged anxiously at his leash.

"What do you mean, what happened to my marriage? Isn't that fairly obvious? Bill left me for someone else. What's left to sort out, besides some his and hers towels?"

Aunt Mavis and Snuffy started walking again, slowly. Rachel followed them.

"That's not what I meant, my dear. I was thinking about several years ago—ten, maybe fifteen—when I first noticed there were problems in your marriage. Oh, nothing I could ever quite pinpoint, but they were there. Things just weren't the same. What happened, Rachel?"

Rachel quickened her pace, moving slightly ahead of Aunt Mavis. "Nothing happened." She kept her eyes straight ahead. "I don't know what you're talking about. You must have been imaginging things. Besides, if you thought there was something wrong all these years, why didn't you say something before this?"

"I suppose because I felt it was none of my business."

Rachel whirled toward her aunt, her hands on her hips. "And what makes you think it's any of your business now? Look, if you want to take over the house, Thanksgiving or Christmas or whatever, that's fine. But as far as my personal life goes, just butt out, all right?"

* * *

Before Rachel opened her eyes the next morning, she heard the rain. She couldn't decide if she was more disgusted because her plans to spend Saturday working out in the garden had been ruined, or because, once again, Aunt Mavis had been right.

She glanced at the clock on her nightstand. Seven-thirty. That meant Aunt Mavis would probably already be up, bustling around in the kitchen. Rachel knew she wasn't up to facing her aunt this morning, but what could she do to avoid her? Shopping, she thought suddenly. I've always loved going shopping on rainy days. It's early, but if I shower and dress right now, I can get down to the mall before anyone else and do some window shopping first. In fact, maybe I'll even treat myself to breakfast somewhere.

Rachel hurried through the shower, then threw on some slacks and a sweater. Just as she reached the bottom of the stairs and turned toward the hall closet to grab her raincoat, Aunt Mavis came in from the kitchen.

"Good morning, my dear. I thought I heard the shower. Are you ready for some breakfast?"

Rachel opened the closet door and pulled out her coat. "Actually, Aunt Mavis, I'm going out for breakfast. And then I thought I'd take your advice and do some shopping."

"That's a wonderful idea, Rachel." Aunt Mavis raised her eyebrows and smiled. "Can't do much else, since it's raining."

Rachel ignored her.

"Would you like me to come with you?" Aunt Mavis asked.

Rachel slid into her coat, then turned and took an umbrella out of the closet. "I don't believe so, Aunt Mavis. Thanks for the offer, though." She headed for the door.

"Have a nice time, dear."

"Thank you. I will."

It was almost eight-thirty when she pulled into the parking lot at the mall. The stores don't open until nine-thirty, she thought. Guess I'll go on in and find some place to have breakfast first.

As she turned down an aisle to find a parking place near the mall entrance, her car coughed and sputtered, then died. She coasted to a stop in the nearest space and glanced at the gas gauge. Oh, no, I forgot to buy gas yesterday. How could I be so stupid? I don't even have a gas can in the trunk. I suppose I'll have to call Aunt Mavis to come and get me.

She sat up straight. "Well, not until I've at least had some coffee." She grabbed her purse and got out of the car, flipping the lock as she slammed the door. Oh, no, my umbrella! she thought, as the rain hit her in the face. She fumbled in her purse for her keys. "Where are they?" she fumed, feeling the rain trickling through her hair and down her neck. She looked through her car window. There was the umbrella on the front seat. And there were the keys—in the ignition.

Rachel's shoulders sagged. I can't believe this! What next? She turned and ran toward the mall entrance, planning to go into the nearest restaurant and use the phone, and hoping not to see anyone she knew.

As she reached the doorway, she kept her head down as a man carrying an umbrella opened the door for her. She ducked in ahead of him, then looked around for the nearest restaurant.

"Rachel? Rachel Webster, is that you?"

Rachel gasped. The man who had held the door for her—it couldn't be! She turned slowly. "Hello, Cal," she gulped, self-consciously pushing her wet, frizzy hair off her forehead. "How are you?"

Cal closed his umbrella and stepped inside the mall. "Well, I'm fine," he grinned. "But you look a little wet. Didn't anyone tell you it was going to rain today?"

Rachel sighed. "Yes. But I didn't believe it."

"So, what in the world are you doing out so early on a Saturday morning?"

Rachel looked into his soft, gray eyes. What was it about those eyes—that smile—that made her feel as if she could tell him anything? She hardly knew him, yet she felt safe when she was with him, protected somehow.

She took a deep breath and shook her head. "I don't know, Cal. I think I should have stayed home in bed today. But when I woke up and heard the rain, I thought I'd come and spend the day at the mall, do some shopping, maybe have some breakfast."

"That's why I'm here, too," Cal said and beamed. "Breakfast, I mean." He pointed off to the right. "Down there—around the corner—they have the best omelets. Have you ever eaten there?"

She shook her head. "I don't think so."

He took her arm. "Well, you're in for a treat. Let's go."

"Oh, Cal," she protested, "I can't go in there. I look terrible. I locked my umbrella in the car, along with my keys." To her horror, tears began to spill down her cheeks. "And I ran out of gas!" She crumpled against his chest as his big arms wrapped around her. "Oh, Cal, I'm so embarrassed. I'm so sorry."

He tilted her chin up with his finger. "Don't be silly," he smiled. "It's been a long time since I've had breakfast with a lady with wet, curly hair. In fact, I haven't had breakfast with any lady in a long,

long time. Besides, I think you look beautiful."

She dropped her eyes in embarrassment.

"And after we've had a nice breakfast, we'll get your car problems all taken care of, all right?"

She looked back up at him. "I can't ask you to do that."

"You didn't. I offered." He reached into his back pocket and pulled out a handkerchief. "Here, wipe your eyes and blow your nose and let's go order the biggest omelets they've got."

She took the handkerchief and dabbed at her face. "Oh, Cal, I don't know what to say."

Cal grinned again. "Don't say anything. Just get me to that restaurant before I starve to death." He helped Rachel slip out of her wet raincoat, then took off his jacket and draped it over her shoulders. "Besides, we'd better get you some hot coffee."

Rachel hugged her coffee cup as they waited for their omelets.

"Feeling better?" Cal asked.

She nodded. "Yes. My teeth have finally stopped chattering. But I must look a sight."

"You're the best looking woman in the place."

Rachel looked around the restaurant. Three old men sat at the counter sipping coffee. A heavyset woman with bleached hair sat in a booth munching a donut and smoking a cigarette. The only other person Rachel could see was their waitress—who looked as though she should have retired after the Depression.

Rachel grinned. "Maybe you're right."

"Of course I am. I'm a lawyer, remember? Lawyers are always right." He winked. "Besides, wasn't it worth running out of gas, locking your umbrella and keys in the car, and getting soaked so you could have breakfast with me? And this one isn't even tax deductible like our lunch was the other day."

"Oh, I certainly don't intend to let you pay." Rachel insisted. "This one's on me. It's the least I can do."

Cal tilted his head and gazed into her eyes. "Well, then, I guess this really is my lucky day, isn't it?"

Their omelets came then, and Rachel tried to keep her hand

from shaking as she passed him the salt. *What in the world is wrong with me? Some guy feels sorry for me and does me a favor, and I start acting like a stupid schoolgirl!*

As they got up to leave, Cal dropped three one-dollar bills on the table. "The tip's on me," he smiled. Then he leaned over and whispered, "Our waitress is probably working her way through college."

They were both giggling as Rachel paid the bill. The waitress shook her tired gray head at them as she handed Rachel her change, then walked over to clear their table. They watched her smile as she stuffed the three dollars into her apron pocket.

"Well," Cal said, as they walked out of the restaurant. "What next?"

"You know," Rachel smiled, "thanks to you, I feel much better now. And I'm sure you have a million things to do besides help me with my car problems. Why don't you go ahead with whatever it was you had planned before you ran into me? I'll call Aunt Mavis to bring me the spare car key. The Auto Club will take care of the gas. You've done enough already."

"Oh, no you don't. You aren't getting rid of me that easily. Haven't you ever heard of that old Chinese custom? Or is it an Indian custom? Anyway, once you save someone's life, you're responsible for them forever. So, now that you bought me breakfast, you're stuck with me."

Rachel laughed. "I hardly think buying you breakfast qualifies as saving your life. And you're not Chinese—or Indian."

"My great-grandmother was part Chippewa—or was it Ottawa? Maybe it was Choctaw. . . ."

They were both laughing now. "All right," Rachel said finally. "If you really want to help me break into my car, I'll let you. But if we get arrested, I expect free legal counsel."

"It's a deal. But before we work on getting your car back on the road, didn't you say you wanted to do some shopping first?"

"Oh, Cal, I certainly don't expect you to have to drag along behind me while I try on clothes and—"

Cal's eyes sparkled. "You mean you're going to be trying on clothes? Hey, this is getting better all the time. Now, you know you can't go choosing new clothes without an unbiased opinion, don't you? This is going to be fun. I'll find a nice comfortable chair somewhere and sit and wait for you to come out and model for me. What do you say?"

"Oh, Cal, I couldn't."

Cal hooked his arm through hers. "You can do anything you want to do, Rachel Webster. Didn't you know that? Come on. Which store first?"

By noon they were loaded down with bags and boxes. "We're going to have to do something with these," Cal mumbled from behind a shoebox. "I can't see to walk to another store. How about putting them in my car before we look at anything else?"

"Actually, I'm all through," Rachel sighed. "In fact, I'm so tired of trying on clothes, I couldn't stand to look at another thing."

"Well, then, why don't I take you home and you can pick up that extra car key? Then we'll go get some gas for your car, and we'll have you back in running order in no time."

"Are you sure you don't mind?"

"I don't mind. Just look in my jacket pocket for my keys and I'll race you to the car."

"But I don't know where your car is!"

"Follow me."

By the time they got to Cal's car and tossed the packages into the trunk, they were both laughing breathlessly. "I'm exhausted!" Rachel exclaimed, falling into the front seat as Cal held the door for her. "But at least the rain has stopped for a while. Maybe the weather will hold until we get back and get my car fixed."

Cal walked around and opened the door on the driver's side. He climbed in beside Rachel. "Well, I don't know about you," he said, smiling, "but I'll never complain about the rain again. It's been a wonderful morning, Rachel."

Rachel flushed. "It has, hasn't it? Thanks for everything, Cal."

"Hey, we're talking like the day's over or something. What do you say we go out and have some dinner somewhere tonight? After all, it's only fair that I get a chance to take you out in one of those new dresses I helped you pick out, right?"

Rachel looked down. "Oh, well, I . . . I don't know if I can."

Cal reached over and tilted her chin up again until she had to look at him. "Have you forgotten already, Rachel? You can do anything you want to, remember?"

* * *

When Rachel walked in the door that night after a late dinner with Cal, Aunt Mavis was waiting for her.

"It's almost midnight," she said. "I was worried."

"Aunt Mavis, really! I'm not a child. You don't have to wait up for me. I only went out for some dinner."

"In the middle of the night?"

"It's not the middle of the night."

Aunt Mavis sniffed and raised her eyebrows, then turned and walked toward the stairs. She stopped halfway up and looked down at Rachel. "Is your . . . friend . . . a Christian?"

"Aunt Mavis, please!"

Rachel went up to her room to get ready for bed. She had just crawled between the crisp, clean sheets when she heard a knock on her door.

"Yes?"

Aunt Mavis opened the door slowly. "May I come in?"

Rachel sighed. "I suppose so, Aunt Mavis. If you promise not to mention my dinner with Cal."

Aunt Mavis nodded and walked over to the chair across from Rachel's bed. "Joan called earlier this evening," she said as she sat down.

"Really? What did she want? Was it something about work?"

Aunt Mavis smoothed the wrinkles of her robe, then examined her fingernails in great detail. "Well, no, not really," she answered carefully. "Actually, she just wondered if you were planning to come to church tomorrow."

"Aunt Mavis, don't start that again!"

Aunt Mavis looked hurt. "Start what, my dear? I'm just telling you what Joan wanted to talk to you about."

"I'm sorry. I guess I'm feeling a bit defensive right now. Go on."

"Well, she says the women's Bible study group has missed you lately, and that position in the Sunday school class is still open. . . ."

"I'm not interested, Aunt Mavis. Look, I took the job at the preschool, but I told Joan then I wasn't ready for anything else. That hasn't changed."

"Well, there was one other thing that she thought you might be interested in. It sounds like something you should check into, Rachel."

Rachel eyed her aunt suspiciously. "What is it, Aunt Mavis?"

"It's a new group for women. They meet on Sunday evenings after service at Joan's house. They've just started getting together in the past few weeks, but they already have about a dozen women. Joan says the meetings are going very well, and she's sure you'd enjoy coming."

"What kind of women's group? What's it for?"

Aunt Mavis straightened her robe again. "Well, it's for women like yourself—divorced or separated—women going through a hard time. They get together and talk out their feelings—you know, a support group, I suppose."

Rachel got out of bed. "Aunt Mavis, I don't mean to be rude or disrespectful, but I'm going to tell you this just once more—stay out of my personal life! This is none of your business—or Joan's, either, for that matter. And I will tell her the same thing as soon as I see her. I have no intention of pouring my heart out to a bunch of silly, emotional women. I'm doing just fine on my own."

She walked over to the bedroom door and held it open. "Good night, Aunt Mavis."

Chapter 9

Rachel sat staring at the fire as the aroma of roasting turkey floated in from the kitchen. *I really should put on another log, and then go see if Aunt Mavis needs any help with dinner.* She sighed and forced herself to get up and walk over to the fireplace.

Snuffy looked up at her from his spot in front of the hearth and thumped his tail, but when Rachel didn't respond, he closed his eyes and went back to sleep. Placing a log on top of the already smoldering one she'd put in earlier, Rachel jabbed at them with the poker until she was sure the fire would continue to burn. Then she turned and walked to the sliding glass door and stood looking outside.

The pool seemed cold and uninviting with the empty chairs scattered around it. Rachel had let the gardener go soon after Bill had moved out. She had always resented seeing him working in the yard. It was as if she were admitting that it was too much for her to do herself. Now that he was gone, she wondered if maybe it was too much for her. She had just cleaned the pool and swept the patio the day before, and now there were several big brown and yellow maple leaves from the tree next door scattered across the yard and floating in the pool. Looking above the brick fence that separated the two houses, she could see the maple tree stretching its almost empty branches into the gray November sky.

She shook her head and sighed again. *Thanksgiving! That's a laugh!* She turned and walked slowly out into the hallway and toward the kitchen. "Need any help, Aunt Mavis?" she called halfheartedly.

Before Aunt Mavis could answer, the doorbell rang.

"I'll get it," Rachel said. "It's probably Chuck and Jenny."

As she opened the door, she was amazed at how pale Jennifer's face was. It was so unusual for Rachel to see her daughter with anything but a rosy complexion. Even Chuck's smile seemed tired and strained.

"Come in, you two!" Rachel smiled as warmly as she could, reaching out first to hug Jennifer, then Chuck. "You must be freezing. Come sit by the fire; I think Aunt Mavis has some hot cider on the stove."

"I certainly do!" Aunt Mavis agreed, coming in from the kitchen with a big smile, a smudge of flour across her cheek. Her face was flushed and she seemed to be the only one radiating any Thanksgiving spirit.

Aunt Mavis hugged everyone, including Rachel. Her eyes were shining as she sent them into the den to sit by the fire while she poured the cider.

"I'll help you, Aunt Mavis," Jennifer offered.

"Oh, don't be silly! I can handle it. Go sit down and enjoy yourselves. Chuck, why don't you turn on the television? There's some great football on today, you know. And just as soon as I finish everything out here, I'll join you. Dallas is playing, and you know how I feel about Tom Landry!"

Chuck grinned. "I sure do, Aunt Mavis. Makes me a little jealous sometimes, to tell you the truth!"

Aunt Mavis giggled and went into the kitchen.

"Do you suppose this means we'll have to eat during half time?" Chuck asked, as they made their way into the den.

"Could be," Rachel smiled. "You know how Aunt Mavis loves her football—especially the Cowboys!"

Snuffy stood up to greet them as they walked in. "Hello, old boy," Chuck smiled, giving him an affectionate pat. Jennifer hugged the dog silently.

Rachel and Jennifer flopped down on the couch with Snuffy at their feet, while Chuck turned on the set. Rachel had never cared for football and had never made any attempt to understand the game. As the announcer's voice filled the room—something about a great "draw-action play"—Rachel tuned him out. She looked over at her daughter, who was staring blankly toward the TV. Chuck had sat down beside Jennifer, putting his arm around her protectively as he leaned back to watch the game. She doesn't look good, Rachel thought. So pale. And those circles under her eyes! She's not sleeping well, I'm sure of it.

"What's the score?" Aunt Mavis asked, walking into the room with a tray full of steaming mugs.

"Fourteen to ten, Dallas," Chuck answered. "But it's only the second quarter—anything can happen."

Aunt Mavis smiled confidently as she passed out the cider. "Dallas will win! We always win on Thanksgiving. It's a tradition."

Rachel watched Jennifer's hands as she reached for her cider. They seemed so thin—and they were trembling slightly. Oh, God, I can't stand to see her hurting this way!

Rachel took her own cup and held it tightly. The warmth felt good as it spread out from her fingertips, and the steam drifting up from the cup smelled delicious. She took a sip. It was hot, but wonderful.

"Oh, no!" Aunt Mavis cried, almost dropping her cup of cider. "A fumble! How could we fumble on third down? I can't believe it."

Chuck grinned. "I told you, Aunt Mavis, it's still early in the game. Anything can happen."

Aunt Mavis sat down in the easy chair across from the couch. "All right, you guys," she ordered, staring at the TV, "there's the two-minute warning. Let's get busy and get that ball back before halftime!"

Rachel closed her eyes. I hate having the TV on when we have company. It makes it almost impossible to visit. Of course, under the circumstances, maybe it's for the best. What are we going to talk about? Bill? The divorce? The baby? Oh, well, maybe Aunt Mavis will keep things going. I suppose we can all talk about football—or at least she and Chuck can, while Jenny and I listen and nod politely. It's a safe subject, anyway.

She sat there with her eyes closed, until she heard Aunt Mavis exclaim, "Well, that's it—halftime! At least it's still fourteen to ten. Now I can start setting the table."

Chuck got up and flipped off the TV. "I'll help you, Aunt Mavis. Besides, I'd like your opinion on Dallas's new running back."

When Chuck and Aunt Mavis had gone, Rachel turned to Jennifer. "How are you, darling? I mean, really. You look so . . . pale. Are you eating and sleeping all right?"

Jennifer nodded. Rachel could see the tears brimming in her eyes. "I'm okay, Mom. Chuck takes such good care of me. It's just. . . ." She shook her head as the tears spilled over onto her cheeks. "Oh, Mama, I miss my baby so! Even though I never held him, my arms feel so empty."

Rachel hugged her daughter and let her cry. "Oh, honey, I know you miss him. I know you do."

When Jennifer's sobs had subsided, she sat back and looked at her mother. "Mom, Chuck and I have been talking. We think we need to get away for a while. The doctor doesn't want me to try to have another baby for several months, and we need something to get our minds off our loss. We thought maybe a change . . . ."

"Where would you go, Jenny?"

"Well, Chuck's folks have been asking us to fly back to Colorado and spend some time with them. I think that's what we're going to do."

"That's a wonderful idea! You haven't seen them since the wedding, and they're such lovely people. When would you be going?"

Jennifer looked down at her hands. "We'd like to go at Christmas, Mom. Chuck has someone lined up to cover for him at church." She looked back up at Rachel. "But we were worried about leaving you. I know it's going to be a hard time for you."

"Oh, Jenny, please, don't worry about me. Aunt Mavis and I will be fine here, I promise. And I'll be so relieved to know that you and Chuck are off enjoying yourselves. Really! I think it would do you both a world of good. And I'd feel just terrible if I thought you didn't go because of me. I want you to go, Jenny. And I don't want you to worry about me for one minute."

"Are you sure?"

Rachel nodded. "I'm sure." She paused. "Have you . . . talked to your father about your plans?"

"Briefly. He came by last week for a little while." She frowned and shook her head. "He feels terrible about what happened. Mom, I . . . I don't think he's as happy with his new life as he pretends to be."

Rachel lifted her head and squared her shoulders. "Well, that's really not our problem, is it, darling?" She stood up. "Let's go see if Aunt Mavis and Chuck need any help, shall we?"

* * *

"So, how was your Thanksgiving?" Cal asked.

Rachel looked across the table at this man who, until recently, she had allowed herself to think of only as her lawyer. Tonight she realized how much she'd missed him over the long Thanksgiving weekend.

She smiled as convincingly as she could. "Nice. It was very nice. Chuck and Jenny were there—and, of course, Aunt Mavis. We ate a lot, watched some football . . . ."

Cal brightened. "Do you like football?"

"Oh, no, not me. I don't even understand it. Aunt Mavis is the real fan, I'm afraid. And, believe me, she takes it seriously!"

"Well, good for Aunt Mavis. I love football. Watched quite a bit of it over Thanksgiving weekend myself." He leaned over and put his hand on top of hers. "You know why you don't like football? Because you don't understand it. I'll bet if someone took the time to explain it to you . . . ."

Rachel shook her head. "It's too confusing, Cal. I'd never understand it. I'm afraid I'm a hopeless case when it comes to sports."

Cal squeezed her hand. "Nonsense! It's really not as complicated as it seems. I'll bet I could teach you."

"I doubt it. I'm afraid I'm not even interested enough to learn."

Cal grinned. "I can see it's up to me to change your mind. What are you doing December fourteenth?"

Rachel frowned. "December fourteenth? I have no idea. When's that?"

"One week from Sunday—eleven days from now. The Raiders are playing the Kansas City Chiefs at the Coliseum in Los Angeles. It's an afternoon game, so it shouldn't be too cold. What do you say?"

"Oh, I don't know, Cal. I've never been to the Coliseum, or to a football game. I'm not sure. . . ."

"Well, I'm sure! I promise you, by the end of the day, I'll have you hooked on the game." He shrugged. "And, if not, we'll at least have had a chance to eat some hot dogs and peanuts and spend an afternoon together. How about it?"

"Well. . . ." She looked into his eyes. "All right," she smiled. "But if I don't like it, no more football talk, okay?"

Cal held up his right hand solemnly. "I promise."

Just then the waitress arrived with their pizza. "Oh, boy, does that smell good!" Cal scooped up a large piece and laid it on Rachel's plate. "A work of art!"

He grabbed a piece for himself, took a big bite and rolled his eyes as he chewed. "Delicious!" he sighed, reaching for his glass of wine. "There's nothing I like better than a good pepperoni pizza, but most people ruin it by dumping all sorts of other stuff on it—pineapple, hamburger, peppers." He took a drink, then set the glass down and looked at Rachel. "You're so easy to be with, Rachel. I'm glad you were free tonight. I missed you while I was at my daughter's for Thanksgiving."

Rachel picked up her Coke and sipped it slowly, not knowing how to answer him. Finally, she asked, "How was your visit with your daughter and her family? Did you have a nice time?"

"Oh, sure. I always have a nice time when I visit any of my kids,

93

Brenda especially. Of course, she lives the closest—up in San Francisco. The other three are scattered all over the country, so I don't see them as often. Brenda and Tom have two kids, so I really enjoy going up there and playing grandpa. I never realized how much I'd enjoy being a grandparent. There's nothing like it, you know."

He stopped suddenly as a flicker of pain crossed Rachel's face. "Oh, Rachel, I'm sorry." He set his pizza down and wiped his hands on his napkin, then reached over and took her hand in his. "I wasn't thinking. Please forgive me."

Rachel looked down at their hands. "It's all right, Cal. Really. I can't expect the rest of the world to stop spinning just because my part of it has caved in."

"How's Jenny doing?" Cal asked gently.

Rachel looked up at him again. "Not well. I'm worried about her. But she and Chuck are going to take some time and go visit Chuck's family in Colorado during the Christmas holidays. I think it will do them both some good to get away for a while. I'll miss them terribly, though."

"Oh, Rachel, I didn't realize your family would be gone for Christmas. I promised Brenda I'd be back up for a few days at Christmas, but I hate to leave you alone at a time like that."

"Aunt Mavis will be there." She tried to smile. "Aunt Mavis is always there. We'll do fine, just the two of us. A nice, quiet Christmas—that's what I need, anyway."

Cal smiled invitingly. "If I promise to be home in time for New Year's Eve, will you reserve it for me? Let's see the new year in together, what do you say?"

"I'd like that," Rachel answered. "I really would."

* * *

As Rachel drove to work the next morning, she was still thinking about her evening with Cal. She had been relieved when she came home to find that Aunt Mavis had not waited up for her this time. Rachel had lain in bed staring at the ceiling, remembering the touch of Cal's hand and the look in his eyes as they made their plans for New Year's Eve. She was glad he hadn't tried to kiss her when he brought her home, because she was sure she would have let him. Football! she thought, as she pulled up in front of the school. Who would ever have thought I'd be looking forward to going to a football game?

"What are you smiling about?" Joan asked as Rachel walked into the office.

Rachel reddened. "I didn't realize I was smiling."

"That's all right. Don't stop! It looks good on you."

Rachel hung up her coat. "I suppose I'm just glad the sun has come back out. It's a beautiful morning."

"It certainly is. We'll be able to take the children out on the playground later on, after the rehearsal, of course."

"They sure are excited about the Christmas pageant, aren't they?" Rachel asked.

Joan's eyes sparkled. "Yes! It seems to be the highlight of every year. And I never get tired of hearing the Christmas story told over and over again—especially by the children."

Rachel nodded. "I love those kids."

"I know you do. It shows. That's why they all love you so much, too. Especially Jeremy." Joan smiled. "His mother says he talks about you constantly at home."

"Well," Rachel said self-consciously, "I suppose I had better get to work."

The children had not yet gone to their classrooms, but were playing in the large fellowship hall of the church. Some were building with blocks in the corner, others were playing "dress-up" in the housekeeping area, while still others made objects of clay at a table in the center of the room. Susan, along with another teacher, Cindy Robbins, walked around the room, checking on the different areas of activities.

Susan waved when she saw Rachel. "Hi! Are you ready for another rehearsal?"

Rachel smiled as she remembered how the rehearsal had

gone on Tuesday. "It was a little like trying to organize a bunch of earthworms, wasn't it?"

Susan and Cindy laughed. "It sure was," Cindy agreed. "Every year I wonder how in the world we're going to pull this thing off, but somehow it always seems to come together without too many major disasters. I just love Christmas, don't you?"

Rachel tried to smile, but she was thinking of Chuck and Jennifer spending Christmas in Colorado, and Cal in San Francisco. She wouldn't even allow herself to think of how Bill would be spending it. This was one Christmas Rachel would be happy to have behind her.

"Miss Rachel, Miss Rachel."

Rachel looked up to see Jeremy hurrying toward her, his big eyes dancing with excitement. "Miss Rachel, I get to be a shepherd."

Rachel swooped him up and his arms went around her neck as he repeated his announcement. "I get to be a shepherd in the Christmas package, Miss Rachel!"

Rachel laughed. "Oh, Jeremy, you mean the Christmas pageant. You're going to be a shepherd in the Christmas pageant."

Jeremy didn't seem to notice Rachel's correction. "I know! And my mommy and daddy and my big sister are going to come and watch me be a shepherd!"

"That's wonderful, Jeremy. I'm sure you'll be a wonderful shepherd."

"Miss Rachel, what's a shepherd?"

Rachel looked over at Susan and Cindy, and they all grinned. "Come on, Jeremy," Rachel said, setting him down beside her. "Let's go find a book about Baby Jesus and we'll look at the pictures while we read the story, okay?"

"Okay!" Jeremy agreed, bouncing up and down. "Can I sit on your lap while you read to me?"

Rachel smiled. "Oh, I suppose so, Jeremy. If you promise to be very quiet and listen to the whole story."

"Oh, I will. I will!" Jeremy's excitement bubbled over.

Rachel took Jeremy's hand and they walked over to the bookshelf near the back door.

"Here's one, Miss Rachel."

Rachel looked at the book Jeremy was holding up to her. "No, Jeremy, that one's about Noah and the ark."

"Oh, goody, can we read it?"

She shook her head. "Not right now. Maybe later, okay?" She turned back to the bookshelf. "Here's one, Jeremy."

They walked over to a bench at the back of the room and sat down. As Jeremy climbed up into Rachel's lap and looked up at her, Rachel took a deep breath and swallowed the familiar lump that seemed to form in her throat everytime she looked into Jeremy's trusting brown eyes.

"I'm ready, Miss Rachel."

Rachel smiled. "All right, Jeremy. Turn the first page."

"Who's that baby? Is that Baby Jesus?"

Rachel nodded. "Yes, Jeremy, it is."

"I wouldn't like to sleep on hay. What does it say on this page?"

"It doesn't say anything, Jeremy. The story starts on the next page."

Jeremy turned the page. "Who are those guys, Miss Rachel?"

"Those are shepherds, Jeremy. That's what you will be in the Christmas pageant."

"Are they good guys?"

"Yes, Jeremy, they're good guys. Do you know what they're doing?"

Jeremy shook his head. "No, but they have a bunch of lambs."

"That's right, Jeremy. That's what shepherds do. They take care of sheep."

"Of lambs, too?"

"Of lambs, too." She smiled. "Just like Jesus takes care of you."

"You mean I'm his lamb?"

"Yes, Jeremy. You're his lamb." She gave him an extra tight hug.

"And he takes care of me? Always?"

Rachel took a deep breath and blinked away the tears. "Yes, Jeremy. Always."

Chapter 10

"Not exactly the greatest neighborhood in the world, is it?" Cal asked, as he pulled to a stop at a red light.

Rachel, warm and comfortable in the front seat of Cal's car, couldn't help feeling guilty as she looked out the window at the run-down, disintegrating buildings around her. Several old men leaned against an abandoned store, talking and laughing as they passed a bottle hidden in a brown paper bag between them, drinking and wiping their mouths on their dirty coat sleeves. A middle-aged woman sat on a bench, gazing blankly at the passing traffic and pulling at her worn sweater in a vain attempt to block out the gray dampness that seemed to hang over the city like a shroud.

Suddenly, Rachel noticed a group of young men, pushing, shoving, and laughing, as they swaggered down the street toward them. When one of them caught her looking at them, he sneered, and she dropped her gaze, resisting the impulse to reach over and lock her car door. She was relieved when the light changed and they began to move once again.

"I had no idea the University of Southern California was in such a depressed area," Rachel commented. "Is this really where the Coliseum is? Where they held the 1984 Olympics?"

"This is it! In fact, you can see the dorms up ahead. We better pull in here and see what kind of parking we can get."

"But it's barely noon. I thought you said the game didn't start until one."

Cal grinned. "That's right. And it's going to be a great game. But when there's this much competition between two teams, the place always fills up fast. You'll be surprised how far we have to walk from the parking lot to the Coliseum. But it's worth it—the Raiders and the Chiefs always play a close game. We'll win, though, of course."

"Which team are we rooting for?"

Cal looked over at her, his gray eyes wide. "You really do have a lot to learn about football, don't you?"

As he pulled into a parking space, Rachel looked up at the sky again. "It's awfully cold out, isn't it?" she asked.

Cal laughed. "For California, maybe. In other parts of the country, football fans sit outside in the snow and rain to watch their teams play. But don't worry—I planned ahead. I brought a blanket." He grinned. "We can snuggle under it and keep each other warm. I probably shouldn't tell you this, but I was hoping for cold weather. It seemed like the surest way to get close to you for a whole afternoon."

Rachel could feel her cheeks burning as she reached for her purse. She wondered if Cal could hear her heart pounding.

Cal got the blanket out of the trunk and draped it over one arm, threw a pair of binoculars over his shoulder, then took Rachel's hand. "Let's go. We've got a long walk ahead of us."

It was a long walk, and a cold one, too. But Rachel didn't mind. She was only conscious of Cal's hand wrapped around hers as they headed briskly across the campus toward the Coliseum.

Rachel was amazed at the size of the stadium. She had seen it on TV during the Olympics, but she'd had no idea how huge it really was. There seemed to be food and souvenir venders everywhere she looked.

"Before we get the hot dogs, let's buy you a program so you'll know what's going on. In fact," Cal grinned, "let's get you a hat so you'll know what team to cheer for."

The next thing she knew, she was wearing a black and silver hat that said "Los Angeles Raiders" on the front, and carrying a program, while Cal ordered hot dogs and coffee. She glanced around at the milling crowds. A person could sure get lost around here! she thought, edging closer to Cal.

"Ready?" he asked, turning to her, his hands full of hot dogs and Styrofoam cups with plastic lids.

She nodded. "Here, let me help you carry something." She took the cups, enjoying their warmth as she held them, and they walked toward a tunnel where an attendant checked their tickets.

Rachel was relieved when they finally got to their seats. They arranged their things around them, and Cal handed her a hot dog. "Hope you don't mind, I put everything on them." He winked. "Except onions, of course."

Rachel reddened again, then looked out at the playing field in front of them. It seemed so far away. How could she possibly tell what was going on?

"I know these aren't the best seats in the place," Cal apologized, "but it's all I could get on such short notice. The binoculars should help, though. And if you have any questions—any at all—just fire away. That's what we're here for, right?"

The hot dogs were delicious, but the coffee had cooled quickly, and by the time they finished eating, Rachel was shivering.

"It's almost kickoff time," Cal explained, looking at his watch. "You see that scoreboard over there? That's going to tell you all sorts of things—what quarter it is, what down, what the score is—so check it often. Meanwhile, just remember—a football field is a hundred yards long. All the teams are trying to do is get the ball from their end of the field to the other end without being stopped by the other team. They get four tries, or downs, to move the ball ten yards or more. If they make it, they get four more downs and try to go ten more yards. If they don't, they have to give up the ball to the other team. If they make it across the goal line they get six points, which is called a touchdown, plus one for what they call the conversion, which is kicking the ball between the goal posts after the touchdown. Or, if they can't run or throw the ball across the goal line for a touchdown, they can kick it through the goal posts for a field goal, which is three points. There's a lot more to it than that, of course, but if you just remember that much and ask questions as you go along, you'll be a pro in no time."

Rachel tried to smile, but her teeth were starting to chatter, and she had no idea what Cal had just said to her. He reached over and took her hand. "Hey, you're really cold, aren't you?" He smiled. "Can't say that I'm sorry!" He unfolded the blanket and spread it across their shoulders, inching closer to her on the bench. He kept his arm around her and leaned over to whisper in her ear. "I like this. How about you?"

Rachel didn't trust herself to speak. She nodded slightly, keeping her eyes straight ahead on the field below. She sat, rigid, not even moving when the teams came out onto the field. As the Raiders were introduced, many around them stood and cheered. Cal and Rachel stayed where they were, although Cal pointed out some of his favorite players to her as their names were called. When he leaned near to speak to her, the warmth of his breath against her neck made her shiver.

"You're still cold, aren't you, honey?" Cal asked softly. He hugged her closer.

Honey, she thought. Dear God, when was the last time Bill called me that? I can't even remember! Her stomach was churning. What am I doing here? This is crazy!

A gust of wind hit them, and she nestled closer against him, amazed at how good his body felt next to hers, and shocked at the thoughts and feelings rising up within her.

"Feeling any warmer?" Cal whispered.

Rachel took a deep breath, glad Cal couldn't see her eyes as she answered. "Yes. I'm doing much better now."

* * *

The teachers and aides sat in the front rows of the church, keeping tight reins on their wiggling, squirming charges. The children kept turning around and peering over the pews, trying to locate their families. The parents were just as bad, craning their necks and pointing and waving. It was almost time for the Christmas pageant to begin.

Jeremy sat next to Rachel. "How do I look, Miss Rachel?" he asked. "Do I really look like a shepherd?"

Rachel looked at him in his red-checkered bathrobe with the piece of red scarf material tied around his head and an old cane in his hand. "You look like a wonderful shepherd, Jeremy. Your mommy and daddy will be very proud of you."

"And my sister, Carrie, too."

"Yes, and your sister, Carrie, too." She smiled and hugged him. "And me, too!"

Jeremy's eyes shone as Joan got up to welcome the families and to start the pageant. Rachel didn't hear what Joan was saying—her mind was on Cal. Had he gotten here yet? Rachel had ridden in early with Joan to help get things set up, but Cal had promised to try to get away from the office in time to see the entire pageant. Rachel had told him so much about the children—especially Jeremy. She wanted him to see where she worked, to meet the children, to understand why she loved her job so much. But most of all, she wanted to see him before he left for San Francisco the next morning.

I can't believe tomorrow's the last Saturday before Christmas! Cal leaves tomorrow, and then Chuck and Jenny on Sunday. It's going to be a long two weeks with the kids gone to Colorado, but at least Cal will be back on New Year's Eve.

"Here I go, Miss Rachel." Jeremy whispered.

Rachel shook her head and looked around her. The shepherds were going up on stage, finding their places in front of the painted backdrop of sheep grazing below a star-studded sky. Jeremy looked at Rachel and grinned. She smiled back as encouragingly as she could.

Before she knew it, the program was almost over, and it was time for the teachers and aides to get up and lead the children in singing. As she stood up and looked out over the audience, there amidst all the proud and anxious parents sat Cal, beaming at her. He waved when she spotted him, and she flushed with pleasure. Two rows behind him sat Aunt Mavis with Chuck and Jennifer. Rachel was sure Aunt Mavis had seen Cal wave, and she could sense her aunt's disapproval, even at a distance. Oh, God, my last evening with Cal before he leaves—don't let Aunt Mavis ruin it!

"Silent Night" came last. Everyone stood and joined the singing. As Rachel looked at the sweet faces of the children, then out at the audience, she thought, It's not supposed to be like this, God. All the Christmases Bill and I spent together, and here I am, thinking about another man, while Bill is off living with a woman half his age who's going to have his child! And poor Jenny—her first Christmas as a married woman, and she not only has to deal with her parents' divorce, she's mourning the loss of her baby, as well. It's not fair, God. It's not right. I never dreamed—

"We did good, huh, Miss Rachel?" Rachel looked down to find Jeremy pulling at her hand. "Didn't we do good, Miss Rachel?"

"You were wonderful, Jeremy. Just wonderful!"

"You must be the famous Miss Rachel we've heard so much about."

Rachel looked up at a tall, sandy-haired man who had walked up beside Jeremy. Before she could answer, Jeremy cried, "Daddy! Daddy, did you see me? I was a shepherd! Where's Mommy and Carrie?"

"We're right here, darling," a tiny blond woman answered. "Of course we saw you. You were a wonderful shepherd!" She offered her hand to Rachel. "Hi, we're Jeremy's parents. I'm Julia Decker, and this is my husband, Mark, and our daughter, Carrie." Julia's eyes were big and brown like Jeremy's and she seemed scarcely bigger than her son.

Rachel took her hand. "I'm glad to meet you. You have a very fine boy here."

"We think so," Mark smiled, reaching down to tousle Jeremy's hair. "And he certainly thinks the world of you—talks about you all the time."

"I'll say he does," Julia added. "He can hardly wait for Tuesdays and Thursdays to come so he can get to school to see you!"

"That's my sister, Carrie," Jeremy announced, pointing at the thin girl with the pale blond hair, hiding behind her mother. "She goes to big school."

"Is that right?" Rachel asked, smiling at Carrie. "What grade are you in, Carrie?"

"First," Carrie mumbled, peeking up at Rachel. "I'm six."

"Oh, my, you really are a big sister, aren't you?" Rachel said. "Jeremy's told me quite a bit about you. I'm glad to get a chance to meet you, Carrie."

Carrie didn't answer.

"Well," Mark smiled, "it's been a big night. I think we'd better get home."

"I suppose you're right," Julia agreed. "These kids are probably exhausted." She looked at Rachel and grinned. "And I'm sure the teachers are."

They turned to leave, then Julia came back. "I want to thank you for what you've been teaching Jeremy about God. I mean, we don't go to church, and it's important to me that my kids learn these things. Jeremy's been asking us to come here to church sometime—we just might. Thanks again."

As Rachel watched them walk away, she saw Cal coming toward her. *God, what a hypocrite I am. How can I teach children about you when I hardly know what I believe about you myself anymore?*

Cal took her hands in his. "Congratulations, Rachel. It was perfect. Everyone loved it."

She shrugged self-consciously. "They'd love anything their kids did. It really didn't have anything to do with me."

"I wouldn't be so sure about that. By the way, you look fantastic in that red dress! I think you get prettier everytime I see you!"

Before Rachel could answer, Aunt Mavis was standing at her elbow. "Well, Rachel, are you ready to leave? Chuck and Jenny and I all rode over together." She glanced at Cal, then back at Rachel. "We'll be glad to give you a ride home."

Rachel pulled her hands away from Cal and looked at her aunt. Chuck and Jennifer had just walked up behind her.

"Wonderful program, Mom," Jennifer said with a smile. "Everything went so smoothly."

"Thank you, darling," Rachel mumbled. Turning back to her aunt, she said, "Uh, Aunt Mavis, you remember Cal Langsford, don't you? My attorney."

Aunt Mavis nodded politely.

"And, Cal," Rachel went on nervously, "this is my daughter and son-in-law, Jenny and Chuck Miller."

"I've heard so much about you," Cal said and smiled, as he shook hands with Chuck and Jennifer. "It's nice to finally meet you."

"Well, Rachel?" Aunt Mavis repeated. "Are you ready?"

"Well, I . . . ." She looked at Chuck and Jenny, then glanced at Cal. He was silent, but his eyes were pleading with her.

She squared her shoulders. "No, Aunt Mavis, you go on. I should stick around and help clean up, and then Cal and I have some . . . things to discuss. I won't be late."

"I'm proud of you," Cal said later, as they walked out to his car. "And grateful. I would really have been disappointed if I couldn't spend some time with you this evening. It's going to be a long twelve days until New Year's Eve. But I promise not to keep you out late—I know you want to visit with Chuck and Jenny before they leave on their trip."

"They're not leaving until Sunday afternoon. They'll be staying with us until then, so I'll have all day tomorrow and part of Sunday to see them." She swallowed hard and took a deep breath. "Besides, I want to be with you tonight. I'll miss you when you're gone."

Her heart was racing. She could hardly believe she'd had the nerve to say it. What would he think now?

Cal didn't answer. He put his arm around her shoulders as he unlocked the car door for her. She slid in, grateful to sit down. Her entire body seemed to be trembling. She clasped her hands together as Cal went around to the other side of the car and climbed in beside her.

He started the car and drove silently for several blocks. "Are you hungry?" he asked finally.

She shook her head in the darkness. "No, thanks. Not at all."

"Anywhere in particular you'd like to go?"

"I don't know. I can't think of anywhere."

He drove a few blocks farther, then pulled up in front of a large apartment complex and shut off the engine. "Rachel, don't be upset with me, but I just didn't know where else to go. This is where I live. I know you don't drink but . . . how about coming up? For a Coke or something. We could talk. . . ."

Rachel closed her eyes as he reached for her hand. He raised it to his lips and lightly kissed her fingertips. "All right," she whispered. "But only for a few minutes."

The apartment was spacious and warm. There were newspapers scattered across the floor and a dirty coffee cup on top of the TV. Comfortable, she thought as she sat down on the overstuffed couch. I like it.

Cal came in from the kitchen with the Cokes. He handed one to Rachel and sat down beside her. "To us," he smiled, holding the Coke up in front of him.

She clinked her bottle against his and took a sip, then set the bottle down on the coffee table, as Cal leaned forward to kiss her. Oh, God, she prayed, as his warm lips touched hers, if you're listening, I hope you can forgive me!

* * *

"It was a nice, quiet Christmas, wasn't it, dear?" Aunt Mavis asked as they sat in the den watching the tree lights blinking on and off.

"Yes, I suppose so, Aunt Mavis," Rachel answered.

"Of course, it wasn't the same without Jenny and Chuck

and . . . ." She cleared her throat. "This is the first time Jenny's ever been away at Christmas, isn't it?"

Rachel sighed, ignoring her aunt's unspoken reference to Bill. "Yes. And I miss her terribly. I just hope this trip helps her. I've been so worried about her lately."

"Jenny will be all right, my dear. I'm sure of it. She's stronger than she looks. And she has a fine husband to help her through it all. It just takes time."

Time, Rachel thought. How much time? How much time does it take for hurts to heal? How much time until you're whole again?

Suddenly, the memories of her wedding day forced their way into Rachel's thoughts. Bill, so tall and handsome! Her parents and Aunt Mavis, all of their friends. I was so young. I thought I had everything. It all seemed so perfect.

She jumped when the phone rang. "I'll get it! I'm expecting a call."

She ran upstairs to her room and closed the door, grabbing the phone by the bed. If it was Cal, she didn't want to talk in front of Aunt Mavis.

"Hello?"

"Rachel?"

"Oh, Cal, I was hoping it was you! How are you?"

"I'm fine. How about you? Did you survive Christmas?"

"Barely. Just barely. When will you be home?"

"I should make it back sometime Wednesday afternoon—day after tomorrow—just in time for our date. We do still have one, don't we?"

"Of course we do. Cal, I miss you."

There was a pause. "I'm sorry I didn't call sooner, Rachel. Things have been . . . well, hectic around here."

"That's all right. I understand. Cal, the roses were beautiful. They arrived on Christmas Eve."

"I'm glad you liked them. See you in two days."

Aunt Mavis raised an eyebrow as Rachel walked back into the

den. "Did you get your call?"

"Yes, thank you, I did."

They stared at each other briefly, then Aunt Mavis reached over to pet Snuffy and commented, "You know, I was just thinking. Today would have been your twenty-fifth wedding anniversary, wouldn't it? Yours and Bill's."

Rachel's jaws twitched as she clenched her teeth tightly. "I was already aware of that, Aunt Mavis. Thanks so much for the timely reminder."

Chapter 11

"Well, don't you look nice!" Aunt Mavis exclaimed as Rachel walked into the kitchen. "Have you decided to come with me to the New Year's Eve service at church? I'm almost ready to go."

Rachel shook her head. "No, Aunt Mavis. I told you I wasn't going, remember? I haven't changed my mind."

"Then why so dressed up? New Year's Eve is hardly a time to put on your best clothes and sit in front of the television set watching everyone else celebrate." Suddenly, her face drew together in an expression of disapproval. "Oh. Your lawyer friend. Is he back?"

Rachel sat down at the table, her back to Aunt Mavis. "Yes, he is. We're going out for a late dinner."

Aunt Mavis sat down next to Rachel. "I see. And when did all this come up?"

"We've had it planned for some time, Aunt Mavis."

"This is the first I've heard of it."

Rachel's head snapped up and she glared at her aunt. "Aunt Mavis!"

Aunt Mavis raised her hands defensively. "All right, all right! I know. It's none of my business." She sighed and shook her head. "I just don't want to see you hurt again, Rachel. You're so vulnerable right now."

Rachel jumped up from the table. "I can take care of myself, Aunt Mavis! I'm not a child."

"Of course you're not, my dear. It's just—"

The doorbell rang and they both stopped and stared toward the entryway. "Do you want me to get it?" Aunt Mavis asked.

"No. I'm sure it's for me."

Rachel's heartbeat was echoing in her ears as she opened the door. It seemed so long since she had seen him. He stood there, dressed in a dark blue suit, looking strong and handsome. Rachel could hardly wait to feel his arms around her.

"Hi," Cal grinned. "You look beautiful, as usual."

Rachel flushed. "Thanks. Come on in. I just need to get my coat and purse."

Cal stepped inside. "It's chilly out there tonight."

"Yes, it is, isn't it?" Dear God, I can't wait to get out of here so we can talk about something besides the weather!

"Good evening, Mr. Langsford," Aunt Mavis said, walking in from the kitchen. "How was your trip?"

"Fine, thank you, Miss Whittaker. And, please call me Cal."

Aunt Mavis didn't answer.

Rachel reached into the closet and grabbed her coat and purse. "Well, maybe we should get going."

Cal glanced at his watch. "Yes, we should. I have reservations for eight, and it's after seven-thirty now." He looked back at Aunt Mavis. "Nice to see you again."

Aunt Mavis nodded. "Good night, Mr. Langsford."

"I don't think your aunt likes me very well," Cal whispered as they walked to the car.

"Oh, don't worry about Aunt Mavis. She's just afraid I'm going to get hurt."

Cal unlocked the door for Rachel, then went around and climbed in beside her. "So, how are you, Rachel?" He took her hand. "I mean, really?"

The touch of his hand sent a shiver down Rachel's spine. "I missed you terribly, Cal. But I'm all right now that you're back."

Cal looked at her for a moment, then let go of her hand and started the car. "Well, if you're as hungry as I am, we'd better get going."

"Where are we having dinner?"

"It's a new restaurant down at the harbor. I made the reservations before I left for San Francisco. I've heard the food is delicious, and we can watch the lights on the water."

Rachel smiled in the darkness. "Sounds wonderful."

They rode in silence, and Rachel was pleased at how comfortable she felt with this man, even when there seemed to be nothing in particular to talk about. That surprised her. During the long ten days he had been away, she had thought of so many things she wanted to say to him. Oh, well, she thought, there's no rush. We have plenty of time to talk . . . and plan.

"Boy, it's a good thing I made reservations," Cal exclaimed as they pulled up to the restaurant. "It's really crowded."

"Oh, it's lovely. What a wonderful place to spend New Year's Eve."

Cal found a parking place, then got out and opened Rachel's door for her. "Here, let me help you with your coat," he offered, slipping it over her shoulders. "The wind gets pretty brisk down here at night—especially this time of year."

His nearness made it difficult for Rachel to breathe. She turned and looked up at him. "I love your eyes," she said suddenly.

Cal swallowed hard. "Oh, Rachel!"

And then his arms were around her and he was kissing her, tenderly at first, then passionately, hungrily, holding her so closely that she soon forgot the restaurant, the parking lot, the people.

Cal let her go and pushed her back gently. "Rachel, I'm sorry. I'm so sorry. The last time . . . at my apartment . . . after what happened . . . Rachel, I promised myself I'd keep things under control, but . . . I'm sorry, I just . . . ."

She put a finger over his lips. "It's all right," she whispered. "There's nothing to be sorry for."

There were tears in Cal's eyes. Finally, he took a deep breath. "We'd better go eat," he said huskily.

They walked slowly, hand in hand, into the restaurant.

"The name's Langsford," Cal told the hostess. "We have reservations for two at eight."

The hostess checked her list. "Certainly, Mr. Langsford," she smiled. "Right this way, please."

Rachel followed the hostess, with Cal behind her. Suddenly, she froze. Cal almost tripped over her.

"What's the matter?" he asked. "Are you all right?"

Rachel nodded, the nervous twitch beginning over her eye. Then she shook her head and hurried after the hostess.

When they were seated and the hostess had left them with their menus, Cal reached across the table and took Rachel's hand. "What's wrong, Rachel?"

"It's Bill," she whispered. "Bill and Sheryl." She nodded toward the front of the restaurant. "They're over there—in the corner."

Cal squeezed her hand. "Oh, honey, I'm sorry. Do you want to leave?"

She shook her head and took a deep breath. "No. No, I'm fine, really. I'd rather just sit here and have dinner. If we leave now they might see us. Besides, I've got to get used to this sort of thing, don't I?"

"I suppose," Cal answered. "Well, if you're sure you want to stay, maybe we should order. What sounds good?"

Rachel let go of Cal's hand and they picked up their menus. She had a difficult time focusing on the words, and her stomach felt so knotted up she wondered if she would be able to eat anything at all. She took deep breaths, willing her eye to stop twitching, and tried desperately to concentrate on choosing a meal.

"I know this place is supposed to specialize in seafood," Cal said, "but that prime rib sounds too good to pass up. I've always loved prime rib, although Edith would never let me order it. She said it wasn't good for me." He stopped. "Sorry. I wasn't thinking. Have you found anything you like?"

She closed her eyes briefly, trying to think of something that she might be able to eat. "I believe I'll have the salmon," she said.

"Good healthy choice," Cal grinned. "You'll probably live to be a hundred."

Rachel appreciated his attempt to cheer her, but she just couldn't seem to respond. Snap out of this! she told herself. You've looked forward to this evening for two weeks—don't let Bill and Sheryl ruin it for you.

"What would you like to drink, Rachel? Coffee? Coke? I hope you don't mind, but I think I'll have a glass of wine."

Rachel shook her head. "Of course I don't mind. In fact, I believe I'll join you."

Cal's mouth dropped open. "What? I thought you had some pretty strong convictions about that."

Rachel shrugged. "Well, it is New Year's Eve. And besides, it certainly won't be the first conviction I've compromised lately." She winced, then reached across the table and took Cal's hand in both of hers. "I'm sorry. I didn't mean that the way it sounded."

"It's all right, Rachel. I understand. I really do."

Their waiter came then, and they ordered dinner. When he brought them their wine, Rachel raised her glass and asked, "How about a toast for the new year?"

Cal picked up his glass and touched it to Rachel's. "Sure," he smiled. He paused as they stared into each other's eyes. "To the new year," he said finally. "May it bring much, much happiness."

Rachel sipped her wine. Cal's toast had not been all she had hoped, but maybe he would be right about the new year bringing happiness—to both of them. She wondered.

"We certainly have a beautiful view from here, don't we?" Cal commented.

Rachel turned and looked out the window at the many small boats docked in the harbor. The myriad lights from the surrounding buildings shimmered and danced on the still, dark waters. Slowly, her mind slipped back to the first New Year's Eve after she and Bill had been married. It had been only two days since their wedding, and they were spending a quiet, romantic honeymoon in Utah. Snow fell softly outside their rented lodge, and they had fallen asleep in each other's arms in front of a cozy fire. Rachel had opened her eyes as the first soft light of dawn had filtered through the windows. The fire had long since burned out and the room was ice cold, but underneath the quilts, snuggled closely beside her new husband, she had felt safe and warm and very, very loved. *I must be the luckiest girl in the whole world!* she had thought, as she turned to awaken Bill with a kiss.

"A penny for your thoughts," Cal said.

Rachel jumped, embarrassed that she'd forgotten for a moment where she was. "You asked me that once before," she said, smiling self-consciously. "Remember?"

"Yes, I do. And I also remember it was the first time I ever saw you smile. I think maybe it was the first time I realized how beautiful you were."

Rachel blushed, then took another sip of wine. She looked at Cal and smiled again. "This is pretty good—makes me feel warm and relaxed. Just what the doctor ordered, I suppose."

Cal smiled back at her. "I'm glad. I want this to be a really special evening for you—for both of us."

"So do I," Rachel agreed, picking up her wineglass again.

The waiter brought their salads, and Rachel was surprised at how good they looked. *Maybe I'm hungrier than I thought.*

As the waiter walked away, she began to giggle.

"What's the matter with you?" Cal asked, grinning at her.

"Pepper!"

Cal frowned. "Pepper? Pepper makes you laugh? It makes most people sneeze."

Rachel laughed even harder, shaking her head. "No, no, no! It's not the pepper—it's the pepper mill—the one he was carrying around like a trophy or something. Didn't you see it? It was huge. I don't know, it just looked so ... so ridiculous." She wiped her eyes and took a deep breath. "It just struck me funny, somehow."

Cal smiled. "Well, remind me to leave him a big tip. I've been trying to think of something to cheer you up all evening, and he does it with a pepper mill." He shook his head, still smiling. "I'll never understand women!"

Rachel drained her wineglass. "Sorry, Cal. Ever since we

walked in here and I saw Bill and Sheryl, I guess I've been pretty poor company, haven't I?"

Cal signaled the waiter for more wine. "It's all right, Rachel. Really, it is. There are some things that still upset me, too."

Rachel took a bite of her salad and watched the waiter approaching their table with two full wineglasses. What things still upset you, Cal? Will you tell me? Should I ask?

She washed down her salad with a drink of wine, then looked over at Cal. "You mentioned Edith earlier. Is that what you meant just now when you said there were still some things that upset you?"

Cal began pushing his salad around the plate with his fork. "Yes, I suppose it is, Rachel."

She reached over and touched his hand. "I'm sorry. I shouldn't have asked."

He looked up at her, his pain evident in his soft, gray eyes. "It's all right. We're going to have to talk about it sometime. In fact, I've been thinking about it all evening. I just didn't know how to bring it up."

Rachel took a big gulp of wine and shuddered as it went down. "Do you . . . do you want to talk about Edith? About your marriage?"

Cal closed his eyes and took a deep breath. "I don't know if I can, Rachel. I just don't know if I can. I love her so much."

Rachel became aware of a faint ringing in her ears. "Love"? Surely he meant to say "loved"! What is he trying to tell me? Her hand shook as she lifted her wineglass to her lips.

"We had such a good marriage," Cal said. "Or at least I thought we did. I must have been such an insensitive clod not to have noticed her unhappiness, her restlessness. I was so shocked when she left me! Especially when she said it had been coming for years. God, I felt like such a fool! I would have done any-thing—anything—to stop her from leaving, but it was too late. She said there was nothing I could do to change her mind, that she had to leave, to get away, to have some time to find out who she was without me. It didn't make any sense to me then, but I guess now, looking back, I can't really blame her. I was so wrapped up in myself and my practice, I took her for granted. And then, one day, that wonderful, beautiful woman just walked out of my life."

Beautiful? Rachel wondered. How beautiful was she, Cal? How wonderful? As beautiful as you tell me I am? More beautiful? More wonderful? More desirable?

"But I always held on to the hope that she might come back someday. People told me I was foolish to do that—that I should get on with my own life. But she never divorced me, Rachel. If she was so sure she was never coming back, wouldn't she have divorced me? At least, that's what I've always thought. That's why I never dated anyone before this. I wanted to be free if she ever came back. But then I met you. . . ."

Rachel couldn't believe her ears. They're not even divorced! Dear God, they're still married.

Cal took her hand. "Everything changed when we started seeing each other, Rachel. Oh, I still thought about Edith, but suddenly I wasn't so sure I wanted to spend the rest of my life waiting around for her to decide to come home. It was you I thought of when I went to bed at night, you I wanted there beside me. But things were happening so fast, Rachel—for both of us— and I had to be sure! I needed that time during the last ten days to be away from you—to think things through, to try and make some sense out of all this. I knew I was breaking all the rules, dating one of my clients—especially one in as vulnerable a position as you. I never intended for things to go as far as they did that night in my apartment, Rachel. But I just couldn't stop myself!"

"And what did you decide?" Rachel whispered hoarsely. "About us, I mean. And about . . . Edith."

Cal shook his head. "Oh, Rachel, I wish it were that easy!" He let go of Rachel's hand and rubbed his forehead nervously. "I care about you so much. But. . . ."

"But what, Cal?"

He didn't answer for a moment, then he closed his eyes and took a deep breath. "Edith came to Brenda's for Christmas. I didn't know she was coming. Neither did Brenda. She just decided to surprise everyone." He opened his eyes and looked at Rachel. "We spent three days together, Rachel."

Rachel made a fist with her left hand, while she clutched her wineglass tightly in the other. "And nights?" she asked.

Cal didn't answer.

Rachel picked up her wineglass and emptied it. "Well, I guess there's nothing more to discuss, is there?" She set down the glass and threw her napkin onto her salad plate. "Excuse me, but I believe I'll call a cab and go home. Happy New Year, Cal!"

Cal grabbed her hand. "Rachel, wait! Please! Let me at least explain the rest of what happened. Then, if you still want to go home, I'll take you. Please."

Rachel hesitated, staring into his eyes, then settled back into her chair. "All right. I'm listening."

Cal continued to hold her hand. "Rachel, I was with Edith, I'll admit that. And, yes, I still love her—in many ways. But she says she's not ready to come home yet. And I don't know how much longer I can wait—or even if I want to anymore! I told her about you, Rachel, about how much I care about you, but she insists she needs more time. I told her I couldn't promise her anymore time. Rachel, I need you. I need you to be patient, to try and understand."

Rachel snatched her hand away from him and stood up, swaying slightly as she stared down at him. "Oh, I understand! Believe me, I understand! You're asking me to keep your bed warm while you make up your mind just who it is you really love. Is that it?"

Her voice was rising now, and people at nearby tables were beginning to look their way.

"Well, I won't do it!" Rachel exploded, slamming her hand down on the table and knocking over a water glass. "I am not about to share you with your wife while you decide what you want. As far as I'm concerned, you've already made your choice.

Now you can just go back home and wait for her—alone!"

She grabbed her purse and ran out of the restaurant, not even noticing Bill's and Sheryl's startled glances as she hurried past them. As she stepped out into the cold night air, she realized she had left her coat in the restaurant. She shook her head, trying to clear her mind. I can't go back in after it, she thought. Oh, where can I get a cab? I've got to get away from here.

"Rachel, wait!"

Cal had come out the door behind her, and when Rachel heard his voice, she began to run. But she was dizzy, and she knew she'd never outrun him in her high heels. She stopped.

"Rachel!" Cal called breathlessly, running up to her. "Rachel, where in the world are you going? You don't even have your coat!"

She took her coat from his hand. "I'm going to find a phone so I can call a cab and go home—where I belong."

Cal shook his head and looked at her helplessly. "Rachel, what can I say to you? What can I do? I'm so sorry! I never meant for our evening to end like this."

"Maybe not," Rachel said, sliding into her coat, "but it did, didn't it? Don't worry, Cal. I don't blame you. This whole thing is my fault. If I hadn't been so foolish . . . ."

"Rachel, don't say that!" He tried to take her in his arms, but she pushed him away. "Rachel, think of that night we spent together before I left for San Francisco. It was so beautiful—"

"It was a mistake. A stupid, ugly mistake! And it won't happen again!"

"Rachel, please, I don't want to lose you!"

She looked into his eyes, and suddenly she felt very, very tired. "Please, Cal, take me home. I just want to go home."

Chapter 12

Rachel felt as if she were climbing out of a deep, dark pit. If only there were someone at the top to help her! She opened one eye, squinting against the early afternoon sun streaming through her bedroom window. *My God, how long have I been asleep?* She reached for the clock on her bedside stand and held it close to her face, struggling to focus on the hands. *Two o'clock! It can't be! I've never slept this late in my life.*

She started to jump out of bed, then immediately lay back down. The room was spinning around her, and she dropped the clock, clamping her hands over her ears to drown out the noise. But the pounding was inside her head, and it wouldn't go away.

Suddenly the events of the previous night began swirling and dancing before her eyes and she groaned, as tears threatened her once again. *No! No more tears. Please, no more tears.*

Her eyes and sinuses felt swollen from all the crying. When Cal had brought her home, she had refused his offer to walk her to the door. She had slammed the car door and run into the house. Then she had hurried up the stairs to her room, locked the door, and cried until she thought she could cry no more.

She rolled over carefully, stiffly, and saw her shoes and purse on the floor beside the bed. She hadn't even bothered to take off her coat or her dress, and had slept all night on top of the covers. Her hands and feet felt cold, and she wondered if she had the strength to get up and take a warm bath.

Slowly, she slipped her legs over the side of the bed and eased herself into a sitting position, taking several deep breaths and trying to concentrate on the bathroom door. *I can make it. If I just* take my time, I can make it!

When she finally lowered herself into the warm, soothing water, she prayed the steam might help clear her sinuses. Lying back in the water, the bubbles up to her neck, she thought how easy it would be to slip under and never come up. No more pain, no more tears. She closed her eyes, wishing she had the nerve.

And then she saw Jennifer's face—her beautiful, sweet daughter—and thought of the loss that she and Chuck had so recently been through. I could never do that to you, my darling. I could never hurt you like that.

She opened her eyes and forced herself to wash and get out of the tub. She toweled dry and put on a clean robe, then looked in the mirror. Oh, Rachel, you look awful!

She held a cool cloth to her eyes, hoping to ease some of the swelling. Finally, she gave up and ran a brush through her hair. I guess this is it! she sighed, still looking in the mirror. This is how I'm going to start the new year.

Feeling dizzy and unsteady, she walked toward her bedroom door. Coffee! That's what I need. Maybe that will get me through the day.

She made her way down the stairs and into the kitchen, and put a cup of water into the microwave, then rummaged in the cupboard for some instant coffee. The jar was almost empty, but there was enough for a couple of cups.

Hugging the cup tightly as the steam drifted up to her stuffy head, she turned toward the den, thinking how nice it would be to sit quietly on the couch and stare out the sliding glass door at the pool. But as she walked down the hall, she heard voices coming from the den. She stopped, listening carefully. She certainly didn't want to see anyone.

And then she realized it was the television she was hearing. She considered returning to her room with her coffee, but she knew she would have to face Aunt Mavis sooner or later.

"Good morning," she said, walking in and sitting down at the opposite end of the couch from Aunt Mavis.

"Good afternoon, my dear," Aunt Mavis answered, eyeing Rachel closely. "Did you have a good sleep?"

Snuffy lay in front of the fireplace. He looked up at Rachel and thumped his tail, but he didn't get up.

"Yes, thank you, Aunt Mavis. I appreciate your letting me sleep so late. I must really have been tired."

Aunt Mavis raised an eyebrow. "Yes, I imagine you were. Did you have a nice time?"

Rachel took a deep breath. "Fine, thank you. How about you?"

"Very nice—as always." She got up and walked over to the TV. "Well, since you're finally awake, I believe I'll turn this up now. I didn't want to disturb you while you were sleeping."

She turned up the volume, and for the first time Rachel realized that it was a football game Aunt Mavis was watching. Rachel closed her eyes. Oh, great! Just what I need.

"I just love New Year's Day!" Aunt Mavis was saying, as she came back and sat down. "I think it's probably one of my favorite holidays. Why, there are football games on all day long, just one right after the other. Of course, wouldn't you know it? Here it is, another beautiful day in southern California, and when the Rose Bowl is televised nationwide, everyone back East, bundled up in front of a fire, sees all these people out here basking in the sun in the middle of winter, and the next thing you know, they pack up and move here. It's true, you know. The Rose Bowl is the reason for our growing population problems! Just once, I'd like the weather to cooperate and be cold and nasty for the Rose Bowl— you know, like it was the day you went to that football game with your friend—then maybe everyone wouldn't be so anxious to move out here to sunny California." She sighed. "Oh, well, mustn't let a little good weather ruin our New Year's celebration, right? I, for one, intend to make the most of the day and watch every single minute of football I can. I hope you don't mind, but I hadn't planned on making much for dinner—maybe some sandwiches—since Chuck and Jenny aren't here. Unless, of course, you're hungry, dear. Are you? Can I fix you anything?"

Rachel's eyes were still closed. Dear God, isn't she ever going to shut up? she wondered. Aloud, she said, "No, thank you, Aunt Mavis. I'm not hungry."

"Well, let me know if you get hungry, my dear."

"If I get hungry, Aunt Mavis, I'm perfectly capable of fixing myself something to eat."

Aunt Mavis looked at her again. "Of course you are, my dear."

Rachel sat there, listening to the announcer rattle on about what a gorgeous day it was for football, and what a close, spirited game was being played. She tried to tune him out, but his voice droned on, building to a crescendo until it seemed to echo throughout the entire room, vibrating every nerve in her body.

"Can't you turn that thing off?" she snapped, jumping up from the couch. "It's driving me crazy!"

Aunt Mavis blinked. "Why, what's the matter, dear? I thought you were beginning to take an interest in football."

"I hate football! And I hate New Year's Eve and New Year's Day and everything that goes with it!" She stopped, trying to slow her breathing, then reached down to the coffee table and picked up her cup. "I'm going to my room, Aunt Mavis. Please, go ahead and enjoy your game."

* * *

Rachel chewed her fingernail nervously, then glanced at her watch for the hundredth time. The plane was thirty minutes late.

Aunt Mavis reached over and patted her hand. "Relax, my dear. They'll be here any minute. The flight schedule screen said their plane had been delayed. It's nothing to worry about. Happens all the time, especially right now with everyone returning home after the holidays. Trust me. Jenny and Chuck are just fine, I'm sure of it. This sort of thing happens all the time."

Rachel sighed, wishing she shared some of Aunt Mavis's confidence. The knot in her stomach had been growing ever since she had first seen the announcement that the plane had been delayed. She had asked the attendant at the gate what the problem might be, but he said he had no idea, only that it had been delayed for one reason or another. "Happens all the time," he had told her, sounding like an echo of Aunt Mavis.

If I hear that one more time, I'll scream! she thought. I just want them to get home safe and sound. Dear God, I've missed them so much! The weather's been so awful back there. What if something happened during takeoff? What if—

"I think that's their plane now!" Aunt Mavis announced, standing up and walking over to the window. "Yes, I'm sure it is."

Rachel was right behind her. "Oh, Aunt Mavis, I hope you're right." She watched anxiously as the huge plane taxied toward them, pulling up to their gate. "Oh, thank God!" she sighed.

It seemed forever before the passengers began streaming through the tunnel and into the building. Rachel clutched her purse, searching the faces, trying to be calm. "There they are!" she cried, hurrying forward.

Jennifer ran into her mother's arms, as Rachel breathed a prayer of thanks. "I was so worried!" she whispered.

Jennifer stood back and looked at her mother. "What were you worried about, Mom? We're fine."

Her smile seemed to light up her entire face, and Rachel was overwhelmed by her daughter's beauty. She's smiling! she thought. How wonderful to see her smile again.

"Well, it looks as if this trip was just what you needed," Aunt Mavis said, reaching over to hug Jennifer. "You look wonderful."

"I feel wonderful," Jennifer agreed. "And you're right. It was what we needed." She looked back at her husband. "Wasn't it, honey?"

Chuck grinned. "You bet it was!" He kissed her, then hugged Rachel and Aunt Mavis. "But it sure is good to be home again."

"So, how are your parents?" Aunt Mavis asked. "I'm just dying to hear all about your trip! Did you take any pictures?"

"Everyone's fine. And, yes, we took pictures—millions of them! We intend to bore you with them for hours."

They all laughed as they turned to walk down toward the baggage claim area. Aunt Mavis and Chuck led the way, while Rachel and Jennifer walked, arm in arm, behind them.

"You look so much better, Jenny!"

"I am, Mama. I really am. I guess I needed to get away, to have some time alone with Chuck, to think about things, to talk. It was great seeing his family again, too. They're such nice people. They send their love, by the way. In fact, they said they'd love to have you come for a visit sometime. You really should, you know. It's so beautiful there. The snow, the mountains. . . ."

Rachel thought again of the snow-covered lodge in Utah where she and Bill had spent their honeymoon, then quickly shoved the memory from her mind.

"So," she smiled, "tell me all about Christmas in the Rockies! Did you chop down your own Christmas tree?"

As Jennifer chattered on, Rachel listened, so relieved to have her home again. By the time they reached the baggage claim area, some of Jennifer's enthusiasm was beginning to rub off on Rachel.

They squeezed into the crowd of people, anxiously watching for their luggage to come along on the giant turntable in front of them. "There's one!" Jennifer cried.

Chuck grabbed it before it could pass by. "There are two more somewhere," he said. "Oh, there they are!"

With their luggage safely in hand, they turned toward the parking lot. Suddenly, Jennifer stopped. "Oh, there's a restroom. I think I'd better make a quick stop before we leave."

Chuck grinned. "I should have known!" He looked at Rachel. "Has she always been like this—stopping at every restroom she passes?"

"Always," Rachel assured him with a smile.

"I'll go with you," Aunt Mavis said to Jennifer.

"Do women always go to the restroom in pairs?" Chuck asked after Jennifer and Aunt Mavis had walked away.

"Always," Rachel repeated. They both laughed.

"You two really look great, Chuck. That mile-high air must have done you both some good."

"It did, Mom. I always enjoy going home for a visit—but I'm afraid I'm really turning into a true Californian. I can't seem to handle cold weather anymore. When I saw the Rose Bowl on TV, with everyone sitting around in jeans and T-shirts, I couldn't wait to get back here and thaw out."

Rachel winced at the mention of the Rose Bowl, but Chuck didn't seem to notice.

"Actually," he went on, "Jenny handled the cold much better than I did. She dragged me outside every day to play in the snow. We built snowmen, made snow angels, went on long walks—I was sure I had frostbite more than once. But Jenny didn't even seem to notice. She just ran and laughed and played like a little kid!" His voice softened. "Just before we left, she said she's going to talk to the doctor about how soon we can try to have another baby."

"I'm so glad, Chuck." Rachel smiled at her son-in-law. "Did I ever tell you what a special guy I think you are?"

Chuck grinned and shrugged his shoulders. "Oh, several times. But you can tell me again if you want to."

Rachel kissed him on the cheek. "Well, it's true. I'm so glad Jenny has you for a husband."

"So am I!" Chuck agreed. He paused for a moment. "How about you, Mom? How are you holding up? Were the holidays tough for you?"

Rachel hesitated. "Oh, I'm fine—really! I'm just anxious to get back to work on Tuesday. The preschool's been closed for the holidays, you know."

"I know that. And I'm glad you have your job. And I know you're looking forward to those classes you'll be starting at the college in a few weeks. But what about the rest of your life, Mom? Are you working through all of that all right?"

"Of course I am, Chuck," Rachel answered quickly. "Why would you ask? Don't I seem to be?"

"I don't know, Mom. I can't really tell. We've never talked about things, you know. I mean, I never wanted to butt in, and I don't want to push you to talk if you don't want to. But I hope you know I'm here, if you ever do need to talk . . . or pray."

Rachel looked into his brown eyes. She knew he was sincere. She knew he wasn't trying to pry, that he only wanted to help. "Thank you, Chuck. I might take you up on that one of these days."

"Well, here we are!" Aunt Mavis announced, walking up behind them. "Let's go find our car and go home."

* * *

As Rachel pulled up in front of the preschool the following Tuesday morning, she breathed a sigh of relief. It was so good to be back. This was the one place she felt that she belonged, that she was doing something worthwhile.

"Good morning," Joan greeted her as she walked through the doorway. "Welcome back."

"Thanks," Rachel smiled, taking off her coat. "It's great to be back."

"How was your Christmas?"

"Oh, fine. Of course, it was just Aunt Mavis and me. Jenny and Chuck flew back to spend the holidays with his family in Colorado."

"Oh, that's right! How did they enjoy their trip?"

"They loved it. I think it was the best thing they could have done. They both seem in such good spirits."

"I'm glad to hear that. I know how worried you've been about Jenny."

"Yes, I have. But I think she's going to be all right now." She grabbed her smock from the peg by the door and slipped it on. "Well, I'd better get out on the playground. I saw the kids out there when I drove up."

Joan nodded. "Yes, and Jeremy has been asking for you all morning. I think he wants to tell you all about what he got for

Christmas." She sighed and shook her head. "Boy, am I glad it's a nice day out. All the kids seem so wound up after the holidays. At least we can let them run off some of that excess energy outside."

Rachel laughed. "I know what you mean. I wish I had just a fraction of it."

Before she had even reached the gate to the playground, Jeremy was charging toward her, his face flushed and his mouth open. "Miss Rachel! Miss Rachel!"

As Rachel opened the gate, he flew into her arms. "Miss Rachel, wait till I tell you what I got for Christmas!"

She knew she should remind him to run only on the grassy areas of the playground, but instead she hugged him close. "Oh, it's good to see you again, Jeremy! Goodness, you're warm! You must have been doing a lot of running and playing already this morning."

"Yeah, and you know what? I got a new Transformer! And you know what else? I got a Gobot and a bike! It gots training wheels!"

"It has training wheels, Jeremy."

"How did you know?"

Rachel laughed. "You just told me, remember?"

"Oh, yeah. And my sister got a new Cabbage Patch doll. She really likes it. But I think it's dumb. Do you think it's dumb, Miss Rachel?"

"I guess it's not dumb if she likes it, is it?"

Jeremy shrugged. "What did you get for Christmas?"

Rachel thought a moment. "Well, let's see. I got some perfume and a new bathrobe, some stationery—"

"What's that?"

"Stationery? That's writing paper."

"Oh. What else?"

She remembered the roses that had arrived on Christmas Eve from Cal. Obviously ordered before Edith showed up! she thought.

"That's all, I'm afraid, Jeremy."

Jeremy shook his head. "Boy, I'm glad I'm not a grown-up. My mom and dad didn't get any good stuff, either."

Rachel chuckled and hugged him again.

"I don't feel so good," Jeremy said suddenly.

She felt his forehead, then set him down and knelt beside him. "Does anything hurt?"

He shook his head. "No. I'm just kinda tired." He scratched his stomach. "And itchy."

Rachel raised her eyebrows. "Maybe we'd better go see Miss Joan, all right?"

"Do I have to? I'd rather play."

"I'll go with you, Jeremy." She took his hand and they walked into the office. "Miss Joan, Jeremy says he's not feeling too well. Nothing hurts, but he's tired. And I think he may have a slight fever." She paused. "His stomach itches."

Joan's eyes widened. "Hmmm. Jeremy, may I take a peek at your tummy? Just for a minute. I promise I won't hurt you."

Reluctantly, Jeremy pulled up his shirt. Rachel and Joan looked at his stomach, then exchanged glances. "Chicken pox," Joan announced. "Happens about this time every year. Spreads like crazy." She walked over to the phone. "Guess I'd better call his parents to come and get him."

Rachel helped Jeremy tuck his shirt back in.

"Am I sick, Miss Rachel?"

She looked at him, his huge brown eyes brimming with tears and his lower lip trembling. "It's nothing to worry about, sweetheart. It's only the old chicken pox. Almost everybody gets them. All it means is that you get to stay home and watch TV and play with your new Transformer and Gobot for a week or so."

"Have you had the chicken pops, Miss Rachel?"

Rachel looked at Jeremy, then over at Joan, who had stopped in the middle of her phone conversation and raised an eyebrow questioningly at Rachel.

"I don't know if I've had the chicken pops, Jeremy. I can't remember."

Chapter 13

"It seems strange taking a walk without Snuffy, doesn't it?" Rachel asked, glancing over at her aunt. She could see their breath in the cold night air.

"Yes, it does," Aunt Mavis agreed. "This is the second time he hasn't wanted to come with us. I hope he's feeling all right."

"I've noticed he's been awfully listless lately. Maybe I should take him to the vet."

Aunt Mavis nodded. "You're probably right. Although I really don't think he's sick—just getting old, like the rest of us."

Rachel sighed. "It's hard to picture Snuffy getting old. He's been around for so long, I just can't imagine life without him. I have to admit, I was dead set against it when Bill brought him home for Jenny, but that dog has become very special to me. I think I'll call the vet tomorrow and make an appointment for him."

They walked on in silence for a few moments, and Rachel found herself thinking about Jeremy. She smiled when she remembered how he'd looked earlier that afternoon when she'd gone to visit him.

"Aunt Mavis, have I ever had chicken pox?"

Aunt Mavis looked at her niece and frowned. "Chicken pox? Good heavens, Rachel, how should I know?"

Rachel shrugged. "Oh, I just thought you might, that's all."

"I'm afraid I don't, dear. But didn't Jenny have them when she was little?"

"Yes, and I wondered then if I'd had them before. Mom said she thought I'd had a light case, but she wasn't sure. When I didn't catch them from Jenny, I assumed Mom was right and I must have had them. But now I'm not so sure. You remember Jeremy, the little boy I've told you so much about?"

Aunt Mavis nodded. "Of course."

"Well, he came down with chicken pox on Tuesday, and when I went back to work on Thursday, I found out that three more kids had been sent home with them. All the other teachers are positive they've had them, but I just can't be sure."

Aunt Mavis smiled and linked her arm through Rachel's. "Well, my dear, since you didn't get them from Jenny, you're probably safe. But if for some reason you do get them, I'll take care of you," she said and laughed. "I'll even fix you chicken noodle soup and buy you a new coloring book so you'll have something to do."

Rachel pulled her arm away. "Very funny, Aunt Mavis!"

Aunt Mavis laughed again. "By the way, is that where you were all afternoon? Visiting Jeremy?"

"Yes. I went out after lunch and bought him a stuffed animal—a lamb. You should have seen it, Aunt Mavis! It's darling—all soft and fluffy! Ever since Jeremy and I talked about the Christmas story and about Jesus taking care of his sheep, Jeremy calls himself Jesus' special lamb. Anyway, I took it over to him this afternoon. He looked so adorable, with little red spots all over his tiny face. And he loved the lamb! Didn't put it down the whole time I was there! I suppose I shouldn't have gone over while he's still sick, but I figured since I'd already been exposed, why not? Besides, I missed him."

"You really care for that little boy, don't you, Rachel?"

"I do, Aunt Mavis. Probably more than I should. But there's just something about him . . . ."

"Well, I'm certainly relieved to hear that it was Jeremy you were with and not that lawyer friend of yours. He hasn't been around much lately, has he?"

Rachel kept her eyes straight ahead. "No, he hasn't."

Aunt Mavis sniffed. "He certainly has made a pest of himself on the phone, though. I was tempted not to tell you he'd called, but I know how upset you get when you think I'm interfering, so I left you his messages. You did find them, didn't you?"

"Yes."

"And?"

"And what?"

"Did you call him back? He sounded desperate to talk to you."

"No, I didn't."

Aunt Mavis smiled. "Good. I don't know what happened between the two of you—and it's none of my business, I know—" she added quickly, "but I must admit, I'm relieved you're not seeing him anymore. I was so worried about you, Rachel. It's just too soon for you to be thinking about another relationship. You're lonely and hurt and—"

"I know what I am, Aunt Mavis. Let's drop it, all right?"

Aunt Mavis shrugged. "All right, my dear."

As they rounded a corner, Rachel stopped, a distant fragrance teasing her nostrils. "What's that?" she asked.

Aunt Mavis stopped and looked back at Rachel. "What's what?"

"That smell. It's—I don't know—I can't put my finger on it. I like it, and yet—it gives me the creeps, you know what I mean? Like some distant memory. . . ."

"Deja vu, my dear. That's all it is."

Rachel sniffed the air again. "I suppose you're right." She turned back to continue their walk, but a vague sense of uneasiness seemed to follow her.

* * *

The cold water closed over her, and she fought her way to the top, gasping for air and fighting the desire to climb back out of the pool and give up. *No, I'm not getting out! I'm not quitting! I've thought about this for a long time, and I'm going to do it!*

She forced one arm out in front of her, pulling it down and around, then the other arm, willing her legs to kick evenly and rhythmically as she sliced through the water. Ten laps! she told herself. Surely I can do just ten laps. When young I could do fifty.

Midway through her third lap, she knew she would never make the full ten. Maybe five! If I can at least do five, I can work my way up to ten, and then—

"Mom! Mom, can you hear me? Mom!"

Rachel stopped swimming, treading water as she shook her head and blinked her eyes. She looked toward the house and saw Jennifer standing there watching her.

"Hi, honey," she called, swimming to the side of the pool. "I wasn't sure if I heard someone or not. What a nice surprise!"

"I thought I'd come down and spend the day with you, if you don't have any other plans. I know I should have called first, but you know how I am about spur-of-the-moment ideas!"

Rachel laughed. "Yes, I do know! And I think it's delightful." She pointed to a lounge chair. "Would you mind grabbing my towel, honey? It's colder than I thought. This January sunshine can be deceiving."

Jennifer handed her mother the towel, and Rachel climbed out of the pool, drying off quickly and then throwing the towel over her shoulders.

"What in the world made you decide to go swimming today, Mom?" Jennifer asked as they walked inside. "You've hardly stuck a toe in that pool for years."

"I know. And I used to be quite a good swimmer. I guess I just got lazy, didn't feel like redoing my hair and makeup and all. Anyway, I've decided I'm going to get back to swimming again. It's wonderful exercise, you know."

"I think it's great, Mom! In fact, I used to worry about you when you never got any exercise. But now, with all that walking you've been doing with Aunt Mavis, and the weight you've lost, you look better in a bathing suit than I do!"

"Oh, that'll be the day!" Rachel hugged her daughter. "But thanks for saying so. Listen, honey, I think I'll run in and take a quick shower and change, all right? I'll only be a minute."

"Sure, Mom. I'll make some hot tea," Jennifer volunteered.

"Oh, that sounds wonderful."

Rachel rushed through the shower and fluffed her hair into place, then slipped into a jumpsuit and went down to the kitchen to look for Jenny.

"Gee, Mom, that was quick!" Jenny exclaimed. "Here, sit down. The tea's ready—chamomile."

"Mmm, my favorite."

"I know. Where's Aunt Mavis today?"

"Oh, she left early to go visit one of her friends from church. Said she'd probably be gone most of the day."

Jennifer wrinkled her nose and smiled. "That means we can spend the day together—just the two of us. I like that."

Rachel smiled back. "How did I ever end up with a daughter like you, anyway?"

"Just lucky, I guess."

The tea was warm and soothing, and Rachel could feel some of the tension of the past couple of weeks draining away as she sat at the kitchen table with her daughter.

"You know, Mom," Jennifer said, "I noticed when I came in that Snuffy didn't even get up to greet me. He was lying in front of the fireplace in the den, but he barely looked up when I went over to pet him. Is he all right?"

Rachel put her cup down. "Honey, I took Snuffy to the vet a few days ago. He's not sick. He's just getting old. It seems to have hit him all at once. The vet said that happens sometimes. He just doesn't have any of his old zip anymore, I'm afraid. Seldom takes walks with Aunt Mavis and me. Just wants to lie around and take it easy most of the time."

Jennifer stared into her tea cup. "Remember when Daddy first brought him home? He was so adorable! Everytime he tried to run, he tripped over his own feet!" She looked at Rachel and shook her head. "I guess I just never thought about Snuffy getting old. I suppose I thought he'd always be the same; you know, just—well, just Snuffy!"

Rachel nodded her head as she reached out and patted Jennifer's hand. "I know what you mean, darling."

Just then the phone rang. "I'll get it." Jennifer said, jumping up from the table. "It's probably Chuck. I forgot I promised to call him as soon as I got here. He must be getting worried by now." She picked up the phone. "Hello? Yes, she is. Just a minute, please. Mom, it's for you. Mr. Langsford."

Rachel shook her head. "Tell him I can't come to the phone right now. Tell him I'm busy. Tell him. . . ." She took a deep breath. "No, just tell him I don't wish to speak to him."

Jennifer looked puzzled, but relayed the message before she hung up.

"I don't understand, Mom. I thought you and Mr. Langsford were getting to be quite an item. What happened?"

Rachel closed her eyes and rubbed her temples with her fingertips. "It doesn't matter, honey. Let's just say we had a difference of opinion about where our relationship was headed, okay?"

Jennifer nodded. "Okay, Mom. Sure. Uh, you want some more tea?"

"I'd love some more, thanks. Oh, and don't forget to call Chuck."

Jennifer poured the tea, then picked up the phone and dialed. "The line's busy. Guess I'll have to try again in a little while."

As Jennifer sat back down, she asked, "Mom, have you talked to Dad lately?"

Rachel's head jerked up and her eyes flashed. "Now, why would I be talking to your father? What could we possibly have to say to each other that hasn't already been said?"

Jennifer shrugged. "Oh, I don't know. I just thought maybe. . . ."

"Have you been talking to him?"

Jennifer tapped her long nails against her teacup. "Well, yes. I mean, I did have lunch with him last week. Not at his apartment, of course! I refuse to go there—or anywhere that woman is! But I miss Daddy, Mom. I have to see him. I just wish he wouldn't keep trying to get me to be friends with Sheryl. I told him that would never happen. And it really upsets me when he refers to the new baby as my brother or sister."

Rachel took Jennifer's hands in her own. "All of this is so difficult for you, isn't it? I don't know who in the world ever thought divorce was only hard on young children, that once the children were grown and gone, it was okay to rip the family apart. It's never okay. It never stops hurting, does it?"

They looked into each other's eyes, and Rachel was sure they were going to end up crying, but the phone rang again, causing them both to jump.

"That's got to be Chuck this time," Jennifer exclaimed, hurrying to the phone. "Hello? Hello? Who is this? Hello?"

Rachel frowned and walked over to the phone, taking it away from her daughter. "Hello?" There was no answer. Rachel slammed the phone down. "Probably just some kids playing around," she said, smiling at Jennifer. But something inside told her it was more than that.

* * *

"You'd better take an umbrella." Aunt Mavis called from the kitchen. "It looks like rain."

Rachel was standing at the closet door, slipping into her raincoat. She reached for an umbrella. "I've got one, Aunt Mavis. Thanks! I'll be back before supper."

She hurried out to the car, eyeing the dark, ominous clouds overhead. I'd better park in the garage when I come home. I think Aunt Mavis is right about the rain.

As she pulled out of the driveway, she remembered the day she had driven to the mall in the rain. She remembered locking her keys in the car, running to the mall to look for a phone, breakfast with Cal. She shook her head. I'm not going to think about him today—or Bill, either, for that matter. I've got to keep my mind on my studies.

136

She sighed. Who would ever have thought I'd be going back to school at my age? Oh, well, Aunt Mavis tells me you're never too old to learn. I just hope she's right.

Rachel had been to the college before the holidays and had gotten her schedule arranged so she could still work the Tuesday and Thursday morning classes at the preschool. She had been reading through the material she'd gotten when she registered, and had decided to get a head start and go down to the library to do a little research. It's been years since I've been to the library to do anything for myself, she thought. I used to practically live here when I was in high school, but since then, the only time I've come was to bring Jenny. I just hope I can handle going back to studying and homework after all these years.

She found a parking place and went inside. Immediately she had the feeling that she should take off her shoes, as if she were on hallowed ground. I'd forgotten how much I love books, she thought, looking around. What a wonderful place to get lost in. She remembered all the years of coming to the library as a young girl, reading the *Boxcar Children, Little Women,* and *Wuthering Heights.* She suddenly felt like a very bad mother for not having read those books to Jennifer.

She found an empty table and sat down, spreading her books and papers out in front of her. At the table across from her sat an older man, slightly balding, with thick glasses. He was engrossed in a book, obviously unaware of the world around him. As Rachel looked at him, she remembered a television program she and Bill had watched many years earlier. The man in the story had looked a lot like the man sitting across from her now. In the story, the man was a quiet, unassuming bookworm, whose wife nagged him incessantly and never gave him a moment's peace to sit and read.

One day, while the old man was downstairs in the vault at the bank where he worked, a bomb was dropped on the city. Everyone was killed except the old man. When he came out of the vault, he went straight to the library, thrilled that he could finally live his life in peace and read to his heart's content. He had no sooner gotten to the library then he tripped, dropping and breaking his glasses. And there he sat, amidst thousands of books, unable to read even one of them.

Bill had thought the program was silly and unbelievable, and he had teased Rachel because she had cried for the old man, and she couldn't explain why. Even now, somehow, looking at the other man at the table reading his book, she thought of Bill and she felt depressed, on the verge of tears.

Suddenly, she jumped, sure someone had spoken to her, but she didn't know who it was, or what had been said. She looked around her cautiously. The librarian sat behind her desk, sorting and stamping a pile of cards, her half-moon glasses perched on her nose. The old man reading the book hadn't moved, nor did he appear likely to any time soon. A young mother sat at a table in the children's section, turning pages and reading to her two children. The little girl seemed caught up in the story, but the boy was wiggling and squirming, obviously more interested in what he could find under the table than what his mother had on top of it.

There was no one else in the library. Rachel shrugged. I must be letting my imagination run away with me. I'd better stop daydreaming and start getting some serious studying done.

She turned back to her books and tried to concentrate, but the little boy had tired of his mother's story and had gotten up from the table. His mother called him to come back, but he ignored her, running across the room toward Rachel. He stopped in front of her table.

"Hello," Rachel smiled. "How are you?"

The little boy didn't answer. He stared at her, wide-eyed, with his thumb in his mouth. His big eyes made her think of Jeremy. I'm so glad he's almost over those chicken pox and will be back at school next week. I've sure missed him. Besides, if I haven't come down with them by then, I'll know I'm safe.

"Jason, you get over here," the little boy's mother whispered loudly, coming up behind him and taking his arm. "What have I told you about talking to strangers? Now, you come back over here and sit down until we've finished the story."

They walked away without a backward glance at Rachel. She sighed and closed her eyes, letting her mind wander. Suddenly, she was back in the church, the one in her dream where Jennifer and Chuck were getting married. She was standing, watching, waiting. She knew he was coming. She braced herself for the touch of his hand on her shoulder. The hair on her scalp tingled and a chill shot down her spine, but the hand didn't come.

She sniffed the air. He was there. Why didn't he show himself? Did he think she didn't know? Did he think she didn't remember? The Old Spice, the leather—she could smell them. There was no doubt this time.

"Rachel."

Her eyes flew open and she gasped, jumping up and knocking her chair over. The mother and her children looked at Rachel curiously. The librarian peeked at her over her glasses, then went back to stamping and sorting her cards. The old man didn't move.

Rachel took a deep breath, then another and another. She turned slowly to look behind her. As she turned, she heard the back door to the library close. She ran to the door, peering out into the grayness where a steady drizzle had begun. She was just in time to see a tall, dark shadow disappear around the corner of the building. I must be losing my mind! she thought. This is crazy. I've got to get myself under control.

She walked slowly back to her table, picked up her chair, and sat down as quietly as she could, determined to put her fears behind her and get back to her studying. After all, it was just a dream, she told herself. I was remembering a dream—that's all. Just a dream. . . .

But the faint, lingering smell of leather and Old Spice whispered that this time it was more than a dream.

Chapter 14

Her eye twitched as she knelt beside the still body. Dear God, please let him be asleep, she prayed, as she reached out to lift his head from the floor. Lifeless, it fell backward against her arm, and she dropped him, her hand flying to her mouth to stifle a scream. He's dead. Oh, my God, he's dead.

"Rachel, are you in here? Oh, there you are. I'm going out for a little while. I shouldn't be long. Can I get you anything from—Rachel, what's wrong?"

"He's dead," she whispered. "He's dead, Aunt Mavis."

Aunt Mavis crossed the room toward her niece. She looked down at the floor and gasped, then knelt down beside Rachel. "Are you sure?"

"He's dead," Rachel repeated.

Aunt Mavis put an arm around Rachel. "Oh, Rachel, I'm sorry. I know how much you loved him."

Trembling, Rachel reached out and ran her fingers through the cool, silky fur. "Oh, Snuffy!" Hot tears began to spill down her cheeks, and she leaned down to hug him, sobbing against his neck. She could feel Aunt Mavis rubbing her back, but soon that stopped, and she knew her aunt had left her alone to say good-bye to Snuffy.

Rachel lost track of how long she had been there, holding Snuffy's body, but her legs were stiff and cramped by the time she felt someone's hands on her shoulders.

"Mom?" The voice was gentle, concerned. "Mom, it's me, Chuck. Come on, Mom, let me help you."

He lifted her to her feet and she turned to him gratefully, welcoming his strong arms around her.

"Oh, Chuck, Snuffy's dead!"

"I know, Mom," he said. "Aunt Mavis called me."

Rachel stood back and looked at him. "Is Jenny with you?"

He shook his head. "I didn't think it was a good idea to bring her along. I'll tell her when I get home."

"You're right," Rachel nodded. "Chuck, what are we going to do?"

"You're going to come with me into the kitchen," Chuck answered. "Aunt Mavis has fixed a pot of tea. You just stay in there with her while I take care of things, all right?"

Rachel sat down next to her aunt at the kitchen table, as Chuck turned to go back into the den. Aunt Mavis had two cups of steaming tea already on the table.

"Are you all right, my dear?" she asked, reaching out to cover Rachel's hand with her own.

Rachel nodded. "I suppose so, Aunt Mavis. It's just . . . ." She fought to keep the tears from starting again, then took a deep breath. "It's just that it was such a shock to walk into the den and see him lying there in front of the hearth, just as he always did, and then to realize he wasn't moving, wasn't responding when I called his name. I knew he hadn't been doing too well lately, but I just never imagined . . . ."

"I know, dear," Aunt Mavis said, patting Rachel's hand.

They sat silently for a moment, sipping their tea. "Well," Aunt Mavis sighed, setting her cup down, "at least we can be thankful that he didn't suffer."

Rachel plunked her cup down so hard the tea slopped over onto the table. "What?" she asked, her eyes flashing. "What did you say?"

Aunt Mavis looked puzzled. "Why, I just said that we could be thankful that he didn't suffer."

Rachel jumped up, scraping her chair across the floor. "I don't believe you! My husband has left me for another woman who is going to have his child, my daughter has lost her baby, a man I was beginning to trust and care for has stabbed me in the back, and now my dog has died! And you're telling me I should be thankful. I suppose that means I should get down on my knees and thank God every night that a typhoon hasn't swept through our home or that I don't have leprosy. Because I sure don't have anything else to be thankful for. The only thing God has done for me lately is teach me that you can't depend on anything. Nothing lasts! Everything changes! What good is faith when you can't count on anything in this world? We're all on our own. Can't you see that? Life is just a bad joke—and the joke's on us."

She turned and ran up the stairs to her room, slamming and locking the door behind her.

* * *

"Good-bye, Miss Rachel!"

Rachel looked over at the playground where Jeremy's little face was crisscrossed by the chainlink fence surrounding the sandbox area. Why do I always feel as if I'm abandoning him when he waves at me through that fence? She smiled. I suppose it's because he looks like he's in jail!

She waved back. "Good-bye, Jeremy. See you next week."

Climbing into her car, she sighed as she turned the key. Thank goodness Jeremy is back at school, and that I didn't end up with chicken pox. What a relief!

She started down the street, squinting against the bright winter sun. What a gorgeous day! I really should go home and get started on some studying, or maybe work on the Valentine cards for the kids. I can't believe it's only nine days until Valentine's Day. But it's such a beautiful afternoon, I feel like playing hooky for a while.

Instead of heading for home, she turned toward town, suddenly wanting more than anything to take a walk through the old park where she and Bill used to go when they were dating. I haven't stopped there in years, she thought. It's a perfect day for it.

The park was deserted as she pulled up and stopped. I should have brought some lunch and had a picnic. Oh, well, I'm not very hungry, anyway. And I really shouldn't stay that long.

She threw her sweater over her shoulders and strolled across the park toward some picnic tables. I remember when there was a fishpond here, she thought. I wonder when they took it out.

She sat down on a bench with the sun directly on her back. Mmm, feels wonderful. You never really appreciate sunshine until February.

The playground across from her was empty except for a small stray dog curled up in the sand beneath the swings. Rachel winced at the reminder of Snuffy, then turned her thoughts to the many mornings she had brought Jennifer here to play when she was little. But when they moved to their new house, Bill had insisted he didn't want Rachel and Jennifer to visit the park anymore.

"That neighborhood's going downhill," he'd said. "Nothing but bums and derelicts hanging around there. It's just not safe."

The memory of his words made her shiver, and she pulled her sweater around her tightly as she glanced over her shoulder. How silly! she thought. What in the world could there possibly be to worry about, sitting in a public park in broad daylight?

She closed her eyes, determined to relax and enjoy a little more time to herself before she headed home. Suddenly, she heard a noise behind her, and she jumped, a feeling of panic rising within her.

"Rachel, is that you?"

She turned to see a tall, dark figure silhouetted against the sun. She couldn't see his face, but she knew the voice. She breathed a sigh of relief. "Hello, Bill."

"What in the world are you doing out here by yourself?" Bill asked. "How many times have I told you this isn't a safe place anymore?"

Rachel shrugged. "I suppose I could ask you the same thing. What are you doing here? I thought you'd be at work."

"Actually, I was," Bill answered, walking around to the front of the bench. "Do you mind if I sit down?"

"Suit yourself."

He sat down carefully about a foot away from Rachel, but he didn't look at her. "We're bidding a job near here—some renovation work—so I thought I'd come down and look at it. Then, I don't know, I just felt like taking a walk, I guess."

"And you ended up here."

He didn't answer at first. "We used to come here a lot—you and I," he said finally.

"I remember."

Bill still didn't look at her. "Things were good then, weren't they, Rachel?" His voice was low and husky. "I've never been as happy as I was then."

"Not even now?" Rachel asked. "With Sheryl?"

Bill turned and their eyes met. "Not even now," he answered.

Rachel looked away, wishing she hadn't decided to come to the park. That's not true, Rachel! she admitted to herself. You're glad you're here, and you know it. It's a small victory, at least, to know she hasn't made him as happy as you once did.

Bill cleared his throat. "I heard about Snuffy. Jenny called. I'm really sorry, Rachel."

Rachel blinked and swallowed. "I miss him."

She felt his hand on hers and she stiffened. "I know you do," Bill said softly. "I do, too."

Rachel pulled her hand away. "At least you've had time to get used to not having him around," she said bitterly. "It's been almost five months now, you know. I doubt you miss him the way I do."

"That's not fair, Rachel."

Rachel laughed. "So what else is new? When's the last time you ran across anything that was fair in this world?" She turned to him and lifted her chin, her eyes narrowing. "And when was the last time you worried about what was fair to anyone else? Just as long as Bill gets what Bill wants, right?"

Bill's shoulders sagged. "I had hoped we could talk, Rachel. There are so many things I would like to talk to you about."

"For instance?"

"Well . . . your job. How's that going?"

"Fine, thank you."

"And school. I heard you've started back to school."

"Yes, I did. I have a class tomorrow, in fact."

"Do you like it?"

"Very much. Next question?"

Bill shook his head. "You're not going to help me at all on this, are you?"

"Why should I?"

"Because we loved each other once, Rachel. Shouldn't that count for something?"

"I always thought so. Apparently, I was wrong."

Bill stood up. "I give up. I can't talk to you. I'm going back to work. Why don't you let me walk you to your car? I don't want to leave you here alone."

Rachel looked at him coolly. "Why not? Leaving me alone is one of the things you do best."

* * *

A cold wind whistled outside Rachel's bedroom window as she lay there, listening to the wind chimes clanging wildly and waiting for the room to get light. Mornings always seemed the worst for her when she hadn't slept well. She doubted she could get back to sleep, but she knew if she didn't she'd be dragging before afternoon. Oh, well, at least it's Saturday and I don't have to go anywhere. I've got a lot of studying to do, though. She sighed. I guess that's all I have to look forward to on Valentine's Day.

She closed her eyes and thought of Cal's phone call on Wednesday. He had sounded so happy when she had answered, so hopeful. But she had refused his invitation for dinner, even though he had practically begged her, assuring her that things were finally over between him and Edith.

"I knew it the minute you walked out of my life," he had told her. "I knew it was you I really loved, and not Edith."

But she had turned him down.

She rolled over and realized for the hundredth time how big and empty her king-sized bed was. I never really wanted this big bed, she thought. I was happy with the one we had when we were first married—when we used to sleep curled up in each other's arms all night. But when we moved into this house, you wanted all new furniture. "No more of those old antiques!" you insisted, remember, Bill? Everything had to be new—and big. Somehow, after we got this bed, we never seemed to sleep close anymore, did we? So many things changed after we moved in here. So many things happened.

She shook her head and blinked back the tears. That was fifteen years ago. I'm not going to think about those things anymore. And then she remembered her meeting with Bill the week before. Had he been thinking of her as he walked toward the park? Is that why he had come? Were the memories of their early marriage haunting him as they did her? Was he regretting his decision to leave her? He admitted he wasn't as happy with Sheryl as he was when he and I were first married, she remembered. Does he wish things were still the way they were then? Is he feeling trapped because Sheryl is pregnant?

Once again the tears threatened to overwhelm her. This time she let them come. Oh, God, why? Why did you let these things happen to us? I thought you were a God of forgiveness and mercy. Why have you let our lives be destroyed this way? Why? Rachel sobbed into her pillow, feeling Bill's absence in bed next to her more keenly than she had since he first left.

The next thing she knew the sun was streaming through her window and she realized she had fallen back to sleep. Her head ached and her eyes felt swollen. The wind seemed to have died down a little, and the wind chimes tinkled pleasantly.

Rachel shuffled to the bathroom and splashed cold water on her face. When am I going to learn to stop crying myself to sleep?

It's not worth it. Now I'll be stuffy and congested all day long.

She slipped into her robe and headed down the stairs toward the kitchen. Even through her clogged sinuses, the aroma of freshly brewed coffee was tempting. She poured a cup and let the steam drift up to her nostrils.

"Good morning, dear," Aunt Mavis called cheerily, walking into the kitchen as Rachel sat down at the table. "I see you found the coffee. How about some breakfast?"

"No, thanks. I'm not feeling too well—my sinuses again."

"You get that quite often in the mornings, don't you?" Aunt Mavis raised her eyebrows. "An allergy, do you suppose?"

Good grief, I can't even cry in the privacy of my own room without her knowing it. "Yes, I suppose that's what it is."

Aunt Mavis poured herself a cup of coffee and sat down next to Rachel. "Probably from all this wind we've been having," she said, smiling.

"Could be." You're a lousy actress, Aunt Mavis. But, then, so am I.

"So, what are you going to do today, my dear?" Aunt Mavis asked, stirring her coffee.

Rachel shrugged. "Oh, not much, really. If I feel better later, I may do some swimming."

"You're getting quite good at that again, aren't you?"

"Well, I'm back up to ten laps—a far cry from what I used to do when I was young, but then I'm not young anymore, am I?"

"Compared to whom?" Aunt Mavis smiled. "You look young and healthy to me. In fact, you look better lately than you have in years. It's good to see you taking an interest in yourself again."

"I may as well. No one else will."

"Oh, I hardly think that's true, dear. Why, look at that lawyer, Cal Langsford. Not that I'm not relieved to see that relationship come to an abrupt end, you understand. But you have to admit, he seems upset about it ending. I think, if it were up to him, he would like very much to pick it up again."

"Well, it's not up to him."

"No, of course not, dear. But the point is, if he's that interested in you, why should you think no one else would be? You're a very attractive woman, Rachel. You're bright and witty—a little temperamental and emotional at times—but, all in all, you have a lot to offer. Not just to a man, either. There's more to life than that, you know."

"I certainly hope so. If not, I may as well give up right now."

Aunt Mavis laughed. "Oh, my dear, you certainly are melodramatic sometimes! Seriously, though, you can find a lot of fulfillment in other areas of life besides romance and marriage. I certainly have. And you're not doing so badly yourself these days, with your job that you so enjoy, and now your studies. Don't limit yourself, Rachel. Life can be quite exciting if you let it."

"I suppose." Rachel drained her cup. "Excuse me, Aunt Mavis. I think I'll pour myself some more coffee and then go into the den and do some studying."

"Certainly, dear. Let me know if you get hungry."

Rachel poured her coffee and nodded. "Sure, Aunt Mavis. Thanks."

She walked into the den, avoiding the spot where she had found Snuffy only a couple of weeks earlier. She picked up her books from the coffee table where she had left them the night before, and pulled a chair over in front of the sliding glass door. I should get out and clean that pool. The wind has blown leaves and trash into the water and it looks terrible. Sometimes I wish I hadn't been so anxious to let the gardener go. The pool and yard are a lot more work than I had bargained for. But with Aunt Mavis doing most of the cooking and housework, I really can't complain.

She sighed and opened a book, trying to concentrate, but the words seemed to run together on the page. No matter how hard she tried to block out everything else from her mind, she could make no sense at all of what she was reading.

She slammed the book shut and got up. Maybe if I get outside and get some fresh air—maybe get that pool cleaned out—

maybe then I'll feel better and be able to get some studying done.

Opening the door, she stepped out into the morning sunshine, shivering under her robe. She pulled it tightly around her and walked over to the pool.

"Rachel? Rachel, where are you?"

Rachel turned back toward the door. "I'm out here, Aunt Mavis," she called. "Out by the pool."

Aunt Mavis appeared in the doorway. "There's someone at the front door for you, dear. A deliveryman."

Rachel frowned. "A deliveryman? What in the world?" She looked down at her robe and slippers. "Oh, Aunt Mavis, whatever it is, can't you accept the delivery? I don't want to go to the door like this."

"All right," Aunt Mavis answered, "but I think you're going to be rather surprised when you see what it is."

Rachel followed Aunt Mavis inside. She could hear her aunt speaking to someone at the front door, but she couldn't quite make out what was being said. She waited in the hallway beside the den.

After a moment, Aunt Mavis came walking down the hallway, carrying a huge bouquet of white gardenias. Even with her congestion, Rachel could smell the almost sickeningly sweet fragrance.

"What an unusual arrangement to send for Valentine's Day!" Aunt Mavis was saying. "And there doesn't seem to be any card. Do you suppose they're from your lawyer friend? He sent roses last time, didn't he? Gardenias hardly seem his style, but then, who else could possibly have sent them?"

Rachel was breathing in short, quick gasps. The room, the flowers, and Aunt Mavis's voice all seemed to be swirling together. Suddenly, everything went black.

Chapter 15

Rachel opened the front door and stepped into the welcoming warmth of the entryway. She wrinkled her nose. "Mmm, what is that smell?" she called out, heading toward the kitchen.

Aunt Mavis turned from her spot in front of the sink and smiled. "Welcome home, my dear. I'm just finishing cleaning up. I'll be right with you. I've been cooking most of the morning."

"So I noticed," Rachel commented, lifting the lid on a pot of bubbling stew. She breathed deeply. "Oh, that's wonderful! Is the oven on, too?"

"Yes, but whatever you do, don't open it. You remember that wonderful bread your mother and I used to make together?"

Rachel's eyes grew wide. "Oh, Aunt Mavis! You know that's my favorite. You haven't made any of that in years."

Aunt Mavis wiped her hands on the dish towel just as the tea-kettle began to whistle. Grabbing a pot holder she filled two mugs with steaming tea. "You're right, my dear," she answered, her eyes twinkling. "And I decided it was about time I got busy and made some again. It's such a cold, dreary day outside—the kind of day that puts me in the mood for this sort of thing."

They sat down together at the table and Rachel unbuttoned her coat, slipping it off and laying it over the back of her chair. "Well, if I'd realized that, I wouldn't have been complaining about the nasty weather all morning. We weren't able to take the kids out to play at all today, and they get so wound up when they have to stay inside."

"I'll bet they do. By the way, how's your little friend?"

"Jeremy? Oh, he's fine—growing like a weed. He always

150

seems to have something new to show me everytime I see him. Right now he's trying to learn to stand on his head." She chuckled. "He's so adorable—just can't seem to keep his feet in the air for more than two or three seconds, but he never gives up. He's really something."

Aunt Mavis smiled. "You were like that as a child. I always thought you were a bit stubborn, but your mother insisted you were just determined. Whatever it was, we never could change your mind once you'd decided something."

Rachel sighed. "Sometimes those days seem like a hundred years ago. I was so idealistic then—especially as a teenager. I thought there was a right way to do things and a wrong way, and as long as you did things the right way, everything would always come up roses." She raised her eyebrows and shrugged. "I guess that's not always true, is it?"

Aunt Mavis didn't answer. She stirred her tea slowly, then looked over at Rachel. "When did all that change, Rachel? When did you begin to lose that idealism? I realize you've had reason to become somewhat cynical, even bitter, these last few months, but didn't it happen before that? What was it? What made you cross the line between black and white? When did you first start living in that gray area?"

Rachel took a big swallow of tea, keeping her eyes leveled on her cup. "I don't know what you mean, Aunt Mavis."

"I think you do, my dear. I know I didn't imagine it. I knew you very well when you were growing up, remember? I didn't have a family of my own. Your parents always included me as part of your family, and I appreciated that." She laid her hand on Rachel's. "I couldn't love you more if you were my own daughter, Rachel. I watched you grow up. I watched you turn into a young woman. And I watched you fall in love with Bill. I worried right along with your parents when you married him with stars in your eyes, but we all hoped so desperately that you would be happy, that the marriage would work out. For the first ten years or so, that seemed to be the case. And then you moved here to this house. That's when things began to change, Rachel. Your mother noticed it, too. It wasn't only in your marriage that we suspected things were different. It was you, my dear. It was subtle, but it was there. Even your appearance changed, remember? That's when you started putting on weight, and you began pulling your hair back in a bun—"

"For heaven's sake, Aunt Mavis! I couldn't be a teenager forever. I just decided it was time I started looking my age, that's all. How long did you expect me to run around with long straight hair, looking like some aging hippie? And so I gained a few pounds. So what? Doesn't everyone as they get older?"

"Now, Rachel, don't get defensive! I'm not criticizing you. You were always a good mother to Jennifer. You always kept your home neat and clean. You were active in church and civic affairs. And the few times you and Bill did things together you gave the appearance of being a happily married, successful young couple. But, Rachel, I know you. And whether you want to admit it or not, something happened—something more than the fact that you moved into this house. I know you never wanted to move here, but it was something else. Something happened to you. What was it? What happened that took the sparkle out of your eyes? What changed you from that idealistic young woman who never doubted the right and wrong of things to a dull, lifeless, middle-aged woman before your time?"

Rachel set her cup down quietly, then stood up, looking down at her aunt. "Aunt Mavis, if you want to stay in this house one more day, don't you ever bring this up again, do you understand?" She picked up her coat from the back of the her chair and walked out of the room.

* * *

"Good morning, Rachel."

"Good morning, Joan. It looks as if it might be a nicer day today than it was on Tuesday. Maybe we'll be able to take the kids out for a while later."

"I hope so. It makes for a long week when we have to keep them in every day."

Rachel hung up her coat and grabbed her smock from its hook. "Just in case, I told the kids they could bring something for 'show-and-tell' today. They always enjoy that."

"They sure do!" Joan agreed. "Oh, by the way, how's it working out with Susan? Is she letting you take a little more control of the class now and then?"

"Yes. She's so helpful, Joan. I really appreciate her. She has much more confidence in me than I do sometimes. But that's just what I need right now."

"You'll make a wonderful teacher, Rachel. And training with Susan will be good experience for you. How are your classes at the college going?"

"Very well. I'm surprised how much I'm enjoying them. I have to admit, though, I was a little nervous at first."

"Well, I can certainly understand that. It's tough going back to school at our age. But you're doing so well with the children that I think you'll be able to teach a class of your own next fall."

Rachel raised her eyebrows. "That soon? But I won't have my degree yet."

"No, but with the classes you said you're planning to take this summer, you'll have the twelve credits you need to be able to teach. You are still planning to go on taking classes next year, too, aren't you?"

"Oh, yes! I want to get my degree, Joan. I am so happy doing this work. It's the one thing in my life that I know for sure I'm supposed to be doing. Does that make sense?"

Joan smiled. "Of course it does, Rachel. And I couldn't be happier for you—and for our school. You're doing a wonderful job."

Rachel's cheeks flushed with pleasure. "Thanks, Joan." She turned and walked out of the office and into her classroom. She had come in early to redo the bulletin board before the children arrived. She looked around the gaily decorated room. Oh, if only I could live my life right here in this room with the children!

153

How would I ever have survived without this job?

She was just putting on the finishing touches when the door burst open and twelve squirming, squealing children bounded in, followed by a smiling Miss Susan.

"Here we are, Miss Rachel," Susan called. "Are you ready for us? We've been playing games in the fellowship hall."

"I'm ready," Rachel answered, grinning. "Shall we sit down in our circle on the rug?"

Rachel and Susan sat in chairs facing each other across the circle, while the children sat down on the brightly colored mats that had been arranged around the rug. Each mat had a child's name on it, and the children delighted in being able to identify their own mats by reading their names.

Jeremy sat on Rachel's right, his eyes shining with excitement as he held a brown paper sack firmly in front of him. Each child had brought a special "treasure" from home to exhibit during show-and-tell time, and Rachel wondered what it was that Jeremy had brought with him that he was so obviously proud and anxious to unveil.

Trista, a quiet, shy little girl on Rachel's left, was the first child to open her bag. She had brought a rolling pin, and silently carried it around the circle, stopping and holding it out to each child, but never saying a word.

"Would you like to tell us about your rolling pin, Trista?" Rachel asked.

Trista shook her head.

"I'll bet that belongs to your mother. Do you help her in the kitchen?"

Trista nodded, then turned to Rachel. "We bake pies."

Susan smiled across the circle at Rachel. Each time they were able to get Trista to say anything seemed a triumph to them both.

As they worked their way around the circle, looking at favorite dolls and dump trucks and picture books, Christopher, a lively little boy with curly black hair, stood up and pulled a raggedy, beat-up looking wig from his paper bag.

154

"This is mine," he giggled. "My mom gave it to me for dress-up." He stuck it on his head and made a silly face, sending them all into fits of laughter as he made his way around the circle. Rachel's heart ached with love and appreciation for these children, each so different, and so very precious.

And then it was Jeremy's turn. As he stood up and reached into his bag, he glanced over at Rachel and smiled. "I brought my most favorite present I ever got," he announced.

Must be the new Gobot he got for Christmas, Rachel thought.

When he pulled his hand out of the bag, carefully clutching the soft white lamb that Rachel had given him when he had chicken pox, Rachel swallowed hard. Tears stung her eyes as she fought to maintain her composure.

"My best friend gave me this," Jeremy said softly, almost reverently. "I named him Jesus."

Several of the kids giggled, but Jeremy didn't seem to notice as he began to walk around the circle. "I named him Jesus because I'm Jesus' lamb, and this is my lamb! We take care of each other."

He stopped in front of each child so everyone could have a chance to touch Jesus. "Isn't he soft?" he asked over and over. "Do you like him?"

Everyone agreed that they liked him very much, and finally Jeremy stopped in front of Rachel, holding the lamb out for her to touch. "Do you like him, Miss Rachel? Do you like Jesus?"

Rachel blinked her eyes rapidly as she reached out to touch the lamb. "Yes, Jeremy, I do. I . . . like Jesus . . . very much."

* * *

Rachel sat curled up on the couch in front of the blazing fireplace, an afghan thrown over her legs and a pile of books sitting on the coffee table in front of her. I've got to get some studying done. I've got a test tomorrow, but I just can't seem to concentrate.

She closed her eyes and remembered the look on Jeremy's face as he held out the lamb to her that morning. Oh, God, are you trying to tell me something? Do you really care enough to try to get through to me?

She opened her eyes and sighed, picking up a book from the coffee table, determined to get some studying done. How often do I get an evening like this all to myself? Aunt Mavis has gone off to some women's thing at church, the house is quiet and peaceful—I've got to take advantage of this and study for my test.

She forced herself to read, taking notes as she went along. After about an hour, she noticed the fire was dying down. She closed her book, carefully marking her place, and walked over to the fire, adding another log and poking it carefully until it blazed once more.

I need a break, she thought. Maybe some tea—or some cocoa. Now that sounds like a great idea.

She walked into the kitchen and put the kettle on, then searched through the cupboards for some instant cocoa. Shoot! We must be all out. Guess I'll have tea, after all.

As she poured the hot water over the tea bag, the faint smell of cinnamon drifting up to her from the cup, she cocked her head to one side. Did I hear someone at the door? It was such a faint knock.

She set her tea down on the table, listening carefully, but everything was still and quiet. She pulled out the chair and started to sit down, then changed her mind. No, I'm sure I heard someone. I wonder why they don't knock again—or just ring the bell?

She walked to the front door, peering out the peephole. Everything was dark. She flipped on the porch light, but still she couldn't see anything.

"Is anyone there?" She waited, but there was no answer. She turned to go back to the kitchen, then stopped. This time she was sure she had heard something—not a knocking exactly, but a tapping, or. . . .

She opened the door. "Who's out there?" she demanded, her voice shaking. "Who is it?"

And then she smelled it—the leather, the Old Spice. "No!" she screamed, slamming the door and bolting the lock. "No! Leave me alone!"

She ran through the house, checking all the doors and windows to be sure they were locked. Oh, Aunt Mavis, the one time I wish you were here!

As she reached the den, she gasped. Oh, my God, the glass door. Please, please, let it be locked.

It wasn't. I must have left it open when I came in from the patio this afternoon, she thought frantically. She flipped the lock and pulled the drapes shut, then ran upstairs to check the windows in the bedrooms.

Her legs were shaking when she finally made her way back down to the kitchen. She sank into the chair and clasped her hands around her teacup. What do I do now? Do I call the police? Should I call Chuck and Jenny? What would I tell them? That I heard something? That I smelled something? They'll be terribly upset. They'd probably jump in the car and drive right down, and then what? Find me sitting here sipping tea? Get a grip on yourself, Rachel. You've got to deal with this alone. You're letting your imagination run away with you again.

She drank her tea slowly, taking deep breaths and trying to relax, while at the same time listening, waiting. By the time she drained her cup, she had convinced herself that she had been overreacting.

She walked over to the sink and rinsed out the cup. A bath, she thought. A nice, hot, relaxing bath. That's what I need. Maybe by the time I get out I'll be able to get back to my studies.

She brushed her hair and washed her face as the tub filled with steaming water. Slipping out of her clothes, she eased herself into the tub, enjoying the luxury of the soft white bubbles all around her. Reaching to turn off the water, she stopped. Was the phone ringing? She couldn't be sure. She shut off the water, then listened again. Everything was quiet.

Oh, well, if it was the phone, whoever it was will call back, I'm sure. She slid down into the warm, soothing water and closed her eyes. This is just what I needed. I let myself get so tense sometimes that I just start imagining all sorts of things.

Suddenly, she jumped. Her ears strained and her heart beat wildly in her chest. She heard a creaking sound—the board in the hallway right outside her room. My God, she thought, someone's in the house! But that's impossible. I locked everything—the doors, the windows, unless . . . .

With horror, she thought of the sliding glass door in the den. She thought she had locked it in time, but what if she hadn't? What if he had already come in before she got there? She stifled a scream as she realized he could have been in the house all this time, just waiting.

She knew she had to do something. She forced herself to climb out of the tub and wrapped herself in her robe, not bothering to dry off first. If she could get to the phone in her room she could call the police. Dear God, she prayed, please don't let him be in my room.

Trembling, she opened the bathroom door slightly and peeked into her bedroom. The door to the hallway was closed. The room seemed empty. She crept silently to the phone at her bedside.

As she lifted the receiver to her ear, the board outside her bedroom door creaked again. Rachel stopped, unable to move or to think. Suddenly there was a knock at the door.

"Rachel? Rachel, are you in there?"

Rachel dropped the phone and ran to the door, yanking it open and throwing her arms around her aunt. "Aunt Mavis, it's you!"

Aunt Mavis pulled away from Rachel and frowned at her. "Well, of course it's me. Who in the world did you think it was?" She shook her head. "You know, my dear, you really shouldn't run around dripping wet like that. You'll catch your death of cold. Why don't you go back into the bathroom and dry off while I put the kettle on, and then I'll tell you all about my meeting. We had such a good turnout. I was really pleased. You know how hard it can be to get enough people to volunteer for anything these days. All you have to do is say the word 'committee' and people disappear right and left. But we had almost twenty people there tonight. Very encouraging, I must say. And almost half of them were new faces—that's even better. It usually seems to be the same few people over and over again who show up to do everything, you know what I mean? I know everyone is busy these days, but sometimes. . . ."

As Aunt Mavis rattled on, Rachel smiled with relief. *I don't care if she talks all night. I've never been so glad to see anyone in my entire life.*

"I'll be right with you, Aunt Mavis," she said, hurrying to the bathroom to dry off.

By the time she joined Aunt Mavis in the kitchen, Rachel's hands had stopped shaking. She had decided not to tell her aunt about her fears. They suddenly seemed so silly now that someone else was there in the house with her. She sipped the tea Aunt Mavis poured her and listened gratefully as her aunt went on about her meeting.

"My goodness!" Aunt Mavis exclaimed finally. "I've been going on and on about my evening and I haven't even asked you about yours. Did you do anything special?"

"No, not really," Rachel answered. "Just a little studying—I have a test tomorrow."

"Oh, well, don't let me keep you from your studies, dear. Go right ahead with whatever you need to do."

"Don't worry, Aunt Mavis. I will. Right now I'm enjoying just sitting here and visiting with you."

Aunt Mavis beamed. "Well, how nice. Oh, by the way, Rachel, you had a phone call just as I was coming in the door."

"Really? I thought I heard the phone, but I had the water running in the tub and I wasn't sure. Who was it?"

"Well. . . ." Aunt Mavis hesitated, then frowned and pursed her lips. "Actually, I'm not sure. I mean, he didn't say. And I'm afraid I didn't recognize his voice. It sounded . . . muffled, or . . . I don't know exactly. Anyway, he just asked if the flowers had arrived. I said they had, and asked who was calling, but he hung up. Rachel, is something going on around here that I don't know about?"

Chapter 16

Rachel slipped her sunglasses on as she stepped out of the classroom into the bright February sunshine. It was unseasonably warm, even for southern California, and the breeze teased her short curls as she made her way across the campus to her car. She laid her books on the front seat and started to slide in behind the wheel, then stopped and glanced at her watch. *Eleven o'clock, and I don't have anymore classes today. In fact, I really don't have anything that I absolutely have to do.* She squinted and looked up at the sun. *It's just too gorgeous a day to waste.*

Locking her books in the car, she slung her purse over her shoulder and headed toward the street. *I'll just walk down to the shopping center and browse around, maybe eat lunch somewhere. My car will be fine here at the college until I get back. Sure am glad I wore some comfortable shoes today.*

She smiled as she passed a young couple lying on the grass under a tree near the edge of the campus. *Where else could you sprawl out on the grass and enjoy this kind of weather at the end of February?* she wondered. *With all my complaining about Ventura getting too crowded, I sure can't imagine anywhere else I'd rather live.* The sky seemed exceptionally blue, without a hint of the brown smog that sometimes made its way over the mountains from Los Angeles, ruining Ventura's otherwise beautiful view of the Pacific. Rachel breathed deeply, thankful for her good health as she strode purposefully down the street.

She stopped at a light, watching the long lines of traffic and wondering where all those people were going in such a hurry. *What a luxury to have the afternoon to do whatever I please!*

The shopping center was just around the corner, and she picked up her pace, thinking suddenly how much fun it would be to go looking for a birthday gift for Chuck. It's hard to believe my son-in-law will be thirty years old next month. She grinned. Jenny's been teasing him about it lately, but he has such a good sense of humor it doesn't seem to bother him. What can I get him to show him how very special I think he is? I know Aunt Mavis is already planning a birthday dinner, but I want to find something really unique to give him. That should keep me busy most of the afternoon. She resisted the impulse to stop at a candy store at the entrance to the shopping center. Instead, she decided to stop in at the lunch counter at one of the stores and have some lemonade. All this walking has really made me thirsty. I'll have something to eat later after I've done some shopping.

The lunch counter was crowded, but she saw an empty seat over on one end. She slid in, glad to sit down for a few moments, and laid her purse in her lap.

"Just some lemonade, please," she said, as the waitress came toward her.

A young woman sat two seats down from Rachel, looking very tired and haggard. Rachel judged her to be about six or seven months pregnant. A little girl sat between the woman and Rachel, wiggling on the seat, trying to make it turn, and kicking her short legs against the counter.

"Joanie, be still," the woman ordered.

The little girl stopped wiggling. "I'm hungry," she complained.

"Your lunch will be here any minute," her mother assured her.

The little girl began kicking her legs again.

"Joanie!"

The waitress came with Rachel's lemonade, and Rachel smiled in thanks, taking a long, cool drink. She could feel someone staring at her, and she turned to look at the little girl. Joanie's big brown eyes reminded Rachel of Jeremy, and she remembered what he had said to her not long after she had started working at the preschool. "I wish I could have you for a grandma." Rachel sighed, thinking of Jennifer and the baby that had been lost to all of them.

"Stop staring," the young woman hissed at her daughter. "It's not polite."

The little girl turned around just as the waitress came with two hot dogs and two glasses of milk. "Oh, goody," Joanie cried, clapping her hands with delight.

Rachel closed her eyes and wondered what her grandchild would have looked like. Blond and stocky like Chuck? Or dark and vibrant like Jennifer?

She caught her breath and swallowed hard, then sniffed the air apprehensively. She couldn't be sure, it was so faint, but she thought she smelled Old Spice after-shave. Don't be ridiculous! she scolded herself, shaking her head and opening her eyes. For heaven's sake, lots of men wear Old Spice. I must really be getting paranoid.

She finished her lemonade and picked up her bill. Walking toward the cash register, she caught herself looking at the men at the counter and in the booths around her to see if any of them were familiar. No one was.

Rachel strolled through the indoor mall, stopping to look in the store windows as she passed. I haven't done this in ages, she thought. It's so relaxing.

She came to a men's clothing store. I wonder if I might find something in here for Chuck? I guess it couldn't hurt to look.

"May I help you with anything?" a well-dressed man asked her as she walked into the store.

"Well, I'm not really sure," she answered. "I'm looking for something . . . a gift . . . for my son-in-law's thirtieth birthday next month. I haven't the vaguest idea what, I'm afraid."

"We're having a sale on some very nice sweaters. They're over there on that table, if you'd care to look."

"Thank you." She made her way over to the table, looking at the many different colored sweaters and trying to imagine how Chuck would look in each one. As she picked up a pale blue cardigan to check the size and price, she stopped, her hand frozen in midair. The smell was stronger this time. Her hand began to tremble as she carefully laid the sweater down and looked up. She saw no one in front of her, but behind her she heard the bell on the door tinkle. She spun around, but no one was there except the salesman who had spoken to her earlier.

"Was someone just in here?" she asked.

The salesman looked up. "Excuse me?"

"I said, was someone just in here?"

"Why, yes, I believe there was. Why?"

"Was he wearing Old Spice?"

The salesman frowned, then sniffed the air. "It does smell like it, doesn't it? But I'm afraid I didn't really notice. I was in the back for a few minutes and just came out again as he was leaving. Is something wrong?"

Rachel took a deep breath. "Did you notice what he was wearing? A . . . leather jacket, perhaps?"

The man shook his head. "I'm afraid I didn't notice that, either. Are you looking for someone in particular?"

Rachel clutched her purse tightly to her stomach as she began making her way toward the door. "No, no one, thank you. Thank you very much."

She hurried out the door and over to a bench where she sank down, her legs shaking as she tried once more to reassure herself that she was only imagining things. But that phone call that Aunt Mavis got asking about the flowers, that wasn't my imagination. And neither were the flowers, for that matter. Dear God, it can't be. It just can't be!

"Well, hello, Rachel. What are you doing here?"

Rachel jerked her head up, her eyes wide with fear.

"Oh, I'm sorry I startled you. You must have been released from class early today. Do you mind if I sit down here beside you for a minute?"

Rachel sighed with relief. "Joan! Of course, please sit down. Aren't you working today?"

164

"Oh, sure. I just ran over here on my lunch hour to see if I could pick up something for Mitch for his birthday. It's this weekend, you know, and, as usual, I've put my shopping off until the last minute. That husband of mine is so hard to buy for. I wish he'd take up golf or something so I'd have an idea of what to get him. Whenever I ask him for suggestions, he just says he doesn't really need anything, but I know if I didn't buy him something he'd be hurt. What are you here for?"

"Well, actually, you were right. I did get out of class early today, and since I didn't have anything pressing to do this afternoon, I decided to take a walk. It's such a beautiful day. Anyway, I ended up here and thought I might as well do some birthday shopping, too. Chuck's birthday is coming up next month and I'm afraid I haven't a clue as to what to get him, either."

"Well, at least you're smart enough not to put it off the way I did. Have you been into that men's store over there yet?"

Rachel gulped. "Yes, yes, I have. In fact, I just came out of there."

"But you didn't find anything? Oh, that's too bad. I was just thinking of going in there to look."

"Well, actually, they have some beautiful sweaters on sale."

"Really? Mitch loves sweaters. Maybe I'll go take a look. Care to join me?"

Rachel looked over at the store. "I don't think so, Joan. Thanks. I think I'll go on up to the sporting goods store and see if I can find anything there."

"Okay. Well, I'd better run so I can get my shopping done and get back to school. See you at work tomorrow."

Rachel watched Joan walk away and go into the men's store. Then she took a deep breath and got up, determined to enjoy the rest of her afternoon. I'm not going to let this silly obsession of mine ruin my day. I'm going to finish my shopping, and then have a nice, leisurely lunch before I head back to my car.

She browsed through the sporting goods store, but didn't see anything that seemed quite right. I think I've lost my enthusiasm for shopping. Maybe I'll just go to the cafeteria and have some lunch. That should make me feel better.

She walked slowly down to the cafeteria, stopping to look into the toy store window. Such adorable things, she thought. Will I ever have a grandchild to buy them for?

Unexpected tears stung her eyes as she remembered the day she and Bill had gone shopping for Jennifer's first birthday. Rachel had wanted to have a quiet, simple celebration. She was sure that Jennifer was too young to understand about birthdays or to appreciate cake and presents, but Bill had insisted on helping Rachel make the cake, and they had spent an entire Saturday picking out expensive birthday gifts that they really couldn't afford, while Rachel's parents baby-sat for Jennifer.

We were so happy then. Remember, Bill? You even admitted it—that day in the park. Aren't you happy now? You'll soon have another child. Will you and Sheryl have as much fun shopping for your baby as we did for Jenny? Will you sit up together in the evenings after the baby is asleep and dream of how things will be when your baby is grown and the two of you are old? Or do you ignore that subject, Bill, because you know you'll be old so much sooner than Sheryl? Will you have the energy to play with your new child the way you did with Jenny when she was little? How Jenny adored you! And how she missed you when you got so wrapped up in your business that you were hardly ever home. Will that happen again? Is all this going to work out for you the way you thought it would? Or are you already regretting your decision? Are you wishing you could turn back the clock and do things differently?

She sighed and moved on toward the cafeteria, walking heavily, wondering if her afternoon outing had been such a good idea, after all. Maybe she should try to catch Joan and see if she could get a ride to the college so she wouldn't have to walk back. Somehow she didn't feel nearly as energetic as she had when she began her walk earlier.

No, I'm sure I'll be fine once I've had some lunch. And even if I don't find a gift for Chuck, it's still a beautiful day, and the walk back to my car will be good for me.

She opened the door to the cafeteria and noticed a sign for the day's special—Swiss steak. Mmm, one of my favorites. Maybe that's just what I need to perk me up.

She found an empty booth and sat down, removing the food from her tray. I should have brought something to read. I always feel so conspicuous sitting in a restuarant by myself.

Pretending to be engrossed in reading the weekly special list on her table, she ate without looking up. As she finished the last of her coffee, her eyes grew large. Oh, no, not again! Please, God!

But there was no mistaking it this time. The smell of Old Spice and leather was much stronger than she had ever noticed it before. My God, he's here! He's right here. I know it. What am I going to do?

She buried her face in her hands, trying to think. Suddenly she was aware that someone had walked past her. She looked up, her jaws clenched, her sweaty palms clasped together tightly.

He was tall with silver hair, a dark leather jacket draped over one shoulder as he hurried toward the front of the cafeteria without looking back. He disappeared out of the front door as Rachel stared after him. Dear God, that must be him. It must be.

She stood up slowly, carefully, leaning on the table for support. Turning to look at the booth directly behind her, she gasped. A bottle of Old Spice sat conspicuously in the middle of the table. I've got to get out of here. What if he comes back for his aftershave? She grabbed her purse and started to run for the front door. Then she stopped. My God, I don't have to run. He's not coming back for it. He left it there intentionally. He wanted me to see it.

Rachel forced herself to walk calmly out the door. She headed for the nearest mall exit, all thoughts of doing anymore shopping for Chuck forgotten. I've got to get out of this shopping center. I've got to get some air or I'm going to faint. Oh, why didn't I bring my car? Leaving the mall, she crossed the parking lot, wondering if she should go ahead and walk back to her car or try to catch a bus. She checked the bus schedule posted at the bench, but there was no bus due to stop there that would take her back to her car for almost an hour. *I can walk there in less than that. Of course, I could call Aunt Mavis. . . . No, that's no good. I had a hard enough time the other night convincing her that there was nothing for her to worry about after she'd had that phone call about the flowers. I'm not sure she believed me, even then. I don't dare tell her about this. Oh, God, why can't he just leave me alone?*

She started walking as quickly as she could, wondering why she suddenly felt so cold in spite of the warm sunshine on her back. *It's like a nightmare, God! Like one long nightmare. Please, please, let me wake up. I don't want any of this to be real. Dear God, you know how long I've been afraid of this very thing. I begged you, God. I begged you. Wasn't it enough that you took Bill from me? And then Jenny's baby? But not this, God. Not this, too. Why? Why, after all these years?*

She hurried around the corner and headed for the stoplight. *Come on, come on.* She pushed the "walk" button repeatedly, but it seemed to take forever before the light changed. When it finally did, she ran across the street and down the block. *Oh, God, let me get to my car. I just want to get to my car.*

She didn't see the large crack in the sidewalk and her foot came down hard, twisting as she fell to the ground. "Oh, no! Not my ankle!"

"You okay, lady?"

She looked up at the two teenaged boys standing beside her.

"Are you okay? Do you need some help?"

Rachel suddenly felt very foolish. "Oh, no, thank you. I'm sure I'm fine, really. I just—" She got up, wincing as she put her weight on her left ankle.

"You sure you're okay?"

She tried to smile. "I'm fine. My car's just down the street there—at the college. I'm sure I can make it that far, thank you."

"Maybe we should walk with you," the taller boy suggested. "We don't mind, do we, Jeff?"

Jeff shook his head. "Heck, no. We'll be glad to help you."

Rachel hesitated. "Well . . . if you're sure. I really would feel better if I had some company. It's awfully nice of you both."

The taller boy shrugged. "No problem. Can you walk on it?"

Rachel took a couple of steps. "I think so, but it might be slow going for you boys."

"That's okay," Jeff answered. "We haven't got anything to do this afternoon anyway. We just got out of school and we were kinda hangin' around, you know?"

Rachel smiled. "Where do you boys go to school? Are you over at the high school yet?"

Jeff nodded. "Yep. It's our first year." He looked at his friend. "Me and Dave have been best friends since first grade. This year we only got two classes together. But we still hang around together when we're not in school."

"That's nice," Rachel answered.

"We're going into the Peace Corps together after high school," Dave explained. "We're not going to get tied down with any girls until we've had a chance to see the world."

Rachel swallowed a giggle. "That sounds like good planning to me."

They moved on down the street slowly, one boy on either side of Rachel. Her ankle hurt more than she let on, but she was determined to make it back to her car.

"There it is," she announced, as they crossed the campus parking lot. "I can't thank you boys enough." She opened her purse. "Will you at least let me give you something for all your trouble?"

"Oh, no way!" Dave exclaimed. "It's no trouble. We don't want any money." He shrugged. "Besides, it's what God would have wanted us to do."

Rachel swallowed. "Are you boys Christians?"

"Yes, ma'am," Jeff answered. "Are you?"

She looked from one to the other, then took a deep breath. "I used to be," she said, "but sometimes, lately, I'm not so sure." She took her keys out of her purse and unlocked her car, then turned back to the boys. "Can I drop you anywhere?"

"No, thanks," Dave answered. "Just drive carefully, okay?"

"I will," Rachel promised. "And thank you both—for everything."

She got into her car and buckled her seat belt as she watched the boys walk away, then started her engine. It's warm in here. I need some fresh air. She opened her front window.

"Rachel."

She heard the voice at the same time that she smelled the now familiar odor of leather and Old Spice. The hair on the back of her neck stood up and her hands froze on the steering wheel. She didn't turn her head, but she could see his dark leather jacket in her rearview mirror.

"Don't be frightened, Rachel. I'm sorry if I've scared you. I know I promised to stay away, but I couldn't—not any longer. Please, Rachel, I just want to talk to you. Please."

Terrified, she pressed down on the accelerator, not knowing where she was going, knowing only that she had to get away. She didn't see the other car coming across the parking lot in front of her until it was too late.

Chapter 17

"Rachel! My God, are you all right?"

She turned her head slowly to the left as her car door was yanked open from the outside, and found herself staring into the greenest eyes she had seen since. . . .

"Michael," she whispered.

The dark brows were knitted together in concern, and the lines on his face were a shock to her, as was his gray hair, but she would have recognized him anywhere.

He touched her hand. "Rachel, darling, are you all right? Are you hurt? Oh, I'm so sorry."

"Michael," she repeated, suddenly overcome with an urge to cry. "Oh, Michael, why did you have to come back?" The tears spilled down onto her cheeks. "I wanted to forget you. I wanted to forget. . . ."

"I know, darling," he answered, smoothing the curls back from her forehead. "I know you did. And I know I promised to leave you alone. But when I found out that you and Bill had . . . well . . . I just thought . . . I hoped that, finally. . . ."

She shook her head. "No! No, you don't understand. It can't be. It just can't."

"Hey, mister, is she okay?"

Michael turned around and Rachel looked up, surprised when she saw the crowd that was gathering around them. "My God, Michael, the other car! Is anyone hurt?" She unbuckled her seat belt and tried to move, then slumped back. She covered her eyes with her hand and took a deep breath. "Oh, my head," she moaned. "I'm so dizzy."

171

"Somebody call an ambulance!" Michael hollered into the crowd, then turned back to Rachel. "Oh, Rachel, if you're hurt I'll never forgive myself."

"The other car," Rachel repeated. "What about the other car?"

Michael looked around him. "Is anyone in the other car hurt?" he called.

"No, no, I'm fine," a young man answered, stepping forward. "I saw her just in time. Fortunately, I wasn't going very fast. Nothing but a little 'fender bender.'" He leaned forward and peered into the car. "What about you, lady? Are you all right?"

"I'm fine, really," she assured him, then looked at Michael. "Please, I don't need an ambulance. I just want to go home."

"You can't, Rachel. You've got to go to the hospital and let them take a look at you."

She moved over slightly as he climbed into the car and sat down on the edge of the seat very close to her, pulling the door shut after him. The smell of Old Spice and leather made her feel light-headed. She remembered her dream and shivered as she felt his warm breath on her neck. It would be so easy to let him hold me, she realized.

"Let me take care of you, Rachel. Please. You know how much I've always loved you. I've never stopped thinking about you—never in all these years! We could be happy, Rachel. I know we could. Don't you remember how good it was for us? Those wonderful mornings we spent together while Bill was at work and Jenny was in school. . . ."

"Stop!" She put her hands over her ears. "Michael, I don't want to talk about it. I'm so ashamed. Oh, God, I knew I'd have to pay someday, but I had no idea how dearly. Michael, I've lost my husband and my grandchild."

"You can't blame that on what happened between us fifteen years ago, Rachel. Whatever happened with Bill or with your grandchild, I can't imagine how that could possibly have anything to do with us. Rachel, we loved each other."

"No, Michael, no!" She stopped, remembering the people who

stood around them, and lowered her voice. "Michael, I'm sorry, but I didn't love you." She looked into his eyes, hating herself for what she was saying, but knowing it had to be said at last. "I wasn't honest with you about our . . . relationship. I let you think all along that I felt the same way you did. I didn't mean to take advantage of you, but you were so handsome, so attentive, so good to me. And Bill was too busy to even notice me anymore. I was so unhappy in our new house, rattling around all day with nothing to do but wait for Jenny to come home from school. And you were so romantic! Do you remember the first time we met, at that outdoor restaurant, the one with all the flowers?"

"Of course I remember. You were the most beautiful woman I'd ever seen. I couldn't believe you were alone."

She looked down at her hands clenched tightly in her lap. "I shouldn't have been there by myself. I was asking for trouble." She looked back at him. "But Bill was gone on business and Jenny was spending the night with my parents—I just had to get out of that house. So I got dressed up and ended up at that restaurant. I told myself I'd have some dinner, enjoy the summer evening under the stars, and then go home. But I sat there, staring at my plate, until I noticed that wonderful smell—the gardenia, the Old Spice, the leather . . . ."

"I never put on Old Spice without thinking of you, Rachel. I know how much you used to like it. And I bought myself a new leather jacket right before I came out here. I guess I wanted to see if you'd remember."

"How could I ever forget? When I looked up that night and saw you standing there in your leather jacket and jeans, with everyone else dressed to the teeth, and you were holding the gardenia—Michael, I couldn't have been more touched if you'd been standing there in a suit of armor!"

"I couldn't help it, Rachel. You were sitting there all alone, looking so beautiful with your long brown hair falling down your back. . . . The next thing I knew, I jumped up and picked that flower, wanting more than anything to pin it in your hair."

"Before the evening was over, you did."

"And before the evening was over, I knew I was in love with you. I still am, Rachel."

Rachel took a deep breath and wiped the tears from her cheeks. "I know that, Michael. Although I had hoped, after all these years, you would have found someone else."

"Well, I did marry, right after you told me it was over between us. Sort of a rebound, I guess. But it didn't work out. I just couldn't forget you. And then, when I read in the paper that you'd filed for divorce—"

"You read it in the paper? You still live here in town? I thought you said you were going to move away—to Texas, wasn't it?"

"I did. But I subscribed to the Ventura paper all those years. I suppose it was my way of keeping in touch. I always dreamed that someday I'd see your name listed in the divorce column, but when I actually did, I couldn't believe it. I was already divorced myself, so I wound up some business things back there and took an extended leave of absence. I've been here since right after the first of the year."

"Why in the world didn't you just call me?"

"I wanted to. I started to many times. But I guess I wanted to be sure there wasn't already someone else in your life." He dropped his eyes. "I'm afraid I followed you a few times. I even came by your house. I got as far as the door and knocked, but I just couldn't face you. I'm sorry, but I didn't know how to approach you after all these years." He looked at her again. "Actually, I did call a couple of times, but as soon as someone answered, I couldn't think of a thing to say. That's why I finally sent you those flowers on Valentine's Day. It was the only way I could think of to let you know I was back and that I wanted to see you again. I hoped you would be as happy to see me as I was to see you." His voice dropped. "I see now I've been fooling myself all along."

They stared at each other, but there seemed to be nothing more to say. Then Rachel heard sirens approaching. As a police car made its way across the parking lot toward them, followed closely by an ambulance, Michael kissed her briefly on the cheek. "You're as beautiful as ever," he whispered, then got out of the car and disappeared into the crowd.

* * *

"Hi, Mom," Chuck called out, peeking through the hospital room door. "Got time for one more visitor?"

Rachel smiled. "I always have time for you. Come on in."

Chuck walked over and hugged her. "Where is everybody? I thought Jenny and Aunt Mavis would be here with you."

"They were. In fact, they haven't left my side all evening. I finally ran them out to get some supper in the cafeteria. If you hurry, you can probably catch them."

"Oh, no, I'd rather sit here and visit with you. I'm just sorry I couldn't get here sooner." He grinned and winked. "Some people will do anything for a little attention."

"Oh, Chuck, I'm so embarrassed. There's not a thing wrong with me. I don't know why the doctor insists I stay in the hospital overnight. I'd much rather go home."

"Well, I'm sure he knows what's best. And one night in the hospital isn't going to hurt you. So, tell, me, what in the world happened? All Aunt Mavis said when she called earlier was that you were all right, but you'd been involved in a minor car accident up at the college."

"There's not much more to it than that. I'm afraid it was all my fault, Chuck. I just wasn't paying any attention to where I was going. Thank God, no one was hurt. The policeman said it was a good thing I was wearing my seat belt."

Chuck smiled. "It's good to hear you thank God for something. I haven't heard you say that very often lately."

Rachel reddened. "I suppose you're right. I've been blaming God for everything that's gone wrong in my life, when I should have been accepting the responsibility myself. All of this—Bill and Sheryl, your baby—it's all been my fault, Chuck. All of it."

"How can you say that, Mom? You didn't have anything to do with Dad and Sheryl. They're grown people; they made their own choices. And as for the baby, that just happened. You can't blame yourself for that." His voice softened and he took her hands in his. "Mom, when are you going to forgive yourself? I don't know what it is you've been beating yourself for all these years—and I don't need to know—but it's time you stopped. If God can forgive you, can't you do the same?"

Rachel felt as if a dam were bursting inside her. She threw her arms around her son-in-law's neck and he held her tightly as she sobbed against his shoulder.

"Feel better?" he asked when she had quieted.

"Yes," she nodded, wiping her eyes. "Much better. Thanks."

Chuck got Rachel a cool cloth to put over her eyes, and they sat talking until the door to Rachel's room opened and Jennifer and Aunt Mavis walked in.

"Hi," Jennifer said and smiled. "Is this a private party or can anyone join?"

"It's open to beautiful women only," Chuck grinned, getting up from Rachel's bed to kiss Jennifer, "so I guess you both qualify."

"Smart answer, my dear," Aunt Mavis chuckled, kissing him on the cheek. "Smart answer."

"That was a short supper," Rachel commented. "Didn't you find anything you liked?"

Jennifer wrinkled her nose. "It all looked like . . . like hospital food! We decided to have some coffee and then get something to eat on the way home."

"Wonderful," Chuck exclaimed. "Does that mean I'm invited?"

Jennifer raised her eyebrows. "Well . . . maybe. If you think you can behave yourself."

Chuck held up his right hand in mock salute. "Scout's honor."

Rachel smiled. "Go on, all of you. Why don't you get out and let me get some rest—and get yourselves something to eat."

"Oh, Mom, we don't want to leave you here by yourself while we run off to eat. We can wait. We're not that hungry, really." Jennifer looked over at Chuck. "Are we, honey?"

Chuck held his stomach and grimaced in pain. "Oh, no, I'm not hungry. Why do you ask?"

Jennifer shook her head. "You're impossible—but I love you anyway."

Chuck winked at Rachel and shrugged. "I'm irresistible."

"You certainly are," Rachel said and laughed.

Aunt Mavis sat down on the bed beside Rachel. "Will you be all right if we leave? I'll be glad to stay if you need me."

Rachel wondered if Aunt Mavis could tell she'd been crying. "I'm all right, Aunt Mavis. I'm just tired, that's all."

"Well, if you're sure . . . ."

"She's sure," Chuck interrupted, looking into Rachel's eyes. "And so am I. She's going to be just fine."

* * *

"Oh, Aunt Mavis, it's so good to be home again."

"Well, it's good to have you back. Are you tired? Why don't you lie down while I put your things away? You should stay off that ankle for a few days, anyway."

Rachel shook her head. "No, thanks, Aunt Mavis. My ankle's fine. And, besides, I've been lying in that hospital bed since yesterday afternoon. Right now I'd like to sit out in the backyard in the sunshine, if you don't mind."

"That's a wonderful idea. It's a gorgeous day."

They walked outside, Rachel limping slightly, and pulled two chairs into the sun.

"Why don't we have lunch out here, Rachel? It's so lovely."

"I'd like that, Aunt Mavis. But not quite yet. Let's sit for a while first, can we?"

"Of course. Are you comfortable?"

"I'm fine, thanks."

They sat quietly, gazing out at the pool, the sun sparkling and shimmering on its surface. There was a light breeze, and Rachel closed her eyes, listening to a bird singing overhead.

"It will be spring soon," Aunt Mavis commented.

"With the exception of a few rainy days, it hardly seems as though we've had winter. Not that I'm complaining," Rachel added. Suddenly she opened her eyes and looked at her aunt. "Aunt Mavis, why didn't you ever get married?"

Aunt Mavis looked startled. "Why didn't I get married? Well, I. . . ." She paused, then frowned at Rachel. "Do you think I devoted my life to teaching because I couldn't find a husband?"

Rachel was embarrassed. "Oh, no, I didn't mean that! I don't even know why I asked. I'm sorry. It's none of my business. I just—"

"It's all right," Aunt Mavis interrupted. "I don't mind talking about it. Many people think that, you know—that I devoted my life to teaching because I couldn't find a husband."

"Well . . . did you?"

Aunt Mavis smiled. "Rachel, I'm not going to tell you that there weren't times—many times—when I wished for a husband and children of my own. You know how much I love children. And I always thought I would have made a good mother."

"Oh, that's true, Aunt Mavis. I always thought the same thing. In fact, I've wanted to ask you for years why you never married and had children, but. . . ."

"I know. When a woman hits a certain age and she's still single, marriage becomes a taboo subject, doesn't it? But I hope you haven't wasted your time feeling sorry for your poor old aunt, my dear. I've had a very rich and full life."

Rachel nodded. "I can tell that. And to be perfectly honest, it puzzles me. I suppose I thought you should feel cheated somehow."

"Cheated? By whom? God?"

"Well, I. . . ."

"I have felt that at times, Rachel. And you know me—being the subtle person I am. . . ."

They both smiled.

"More than once I've let God have it with both barrels. I've cried, I've hollered, I've questioned, but always it comes back to the same thing."

"What's that, Aunt Mavis?"

"That he knows what's best for me. That he has his reasons, and whether I ever understand them or not, I still must trust him. You know, Rachel, he's never let me down, never in all these years. He's always been there for me. He's always met my every need. The rewards I've gained through serving him have far outweighed any sacrifices I may have made along the way."

Rachel shook her head. "If only my faith were as strong as yours."

"You have a lot more faith than you realize, my dear."

"But, Aunt Mavis, I don't understand." She hung her head. "Oh, I know there were times I did things I shouldn't have...." She looked back up. "But how long do I have to pay for those things? I tried to make it all up. I tried to be the best wife and mother I possibly could be. I dressed modestly, and never looked at another man again—"

She stopped, horrified at having said as much as she did. "Oh, Aunt Mavis," she moaned, burying her head in her hands. "I'm so ashamed. You were right, all those times you asked about what had happened to change me fifteen years ago—there was something—something terrible. I just couldn't admit it—not even to myself."

Aunt Mavis reached over and patted her shoulder. "It doesn't matter, dear. All that's in the past. It's over, Rachel. Let it die. Bury it, and then go on with your life."

"But, Aunt Mavis, how can God ever forgive me for what I did? I can't even forgive myself."

Aunt Mavis tilted Rachel's chin up, but Rachel dropped her eyes.

"Look at me, Rachel."

Slowly, Rachel looked up.

"Rachel, God doesn't need to forgive you. He already has. He forgave you when he sent his Son to die for you. And if he forgave you then, do you think he's changed his mind now? Do you really think you could have done anything so awful that Jesus' death on the cross wasn't enough to cover it?"

Rachel was silent for a moment. "I hadn't thought of it that way."

"Of course you haven't. You've been thinking that you're the worst sinner—the worst hypocrite—that ever lived, and that everything bad that happened to you was just what you deserved. Isn't that right?"

Rachel nodded. "Yes."

"Let it go, Rachel. Accept his forgiveness—and his love. He's just waiting for you to come to him. You know that, don't you?"

"I always thought I knew it. I mean, I've know Jesus since I was a little girl. I've grown up in the church. I always believed that Jesus died for my sins, and that he rose again, but . . . I guess I just lost sight of it somehow."

Aunt Mavis smiled. "It's easy to do. When we keep looking at our sin instead of at Jesus, the sin seems to grow until we forget that God's forgiveness is bigger than any sin we could ever imagine. There is nothing greater or more powerful than the love of Jesus Christ in our lives, Rachel. Think about that. Hang on to that. And remember what it says above the altar at church: 'Jesus Christ is the same yesterday and today and forever.' When everything falls apart, when everyone you've ever loved and depended on lets you down, remember that he will never let you down. He will never leave you or forsake you. He will never stop loving you because he never, never changes."

Rachel sat silently for a moment, then smiled slightly. "Aunt Mavis, you fell in love with him a long time ago, didn't you?"

Aunt Mavis took a deep breath, and Rachel thought she saw a hint of tears in her aunt's eyes. "Many years ago, my dear. Many, many years ago. And after the love I've shared with him, anything else would have paled by comparison."

Chapter 18

Rachel woke up early the next morning feeling slightly stiff, but rested from a good night's sleep. Yawning and stretching, she rolled over and sat up on the edge of her bed. Think I'll take a shower and wash my hair before breakfast, and then spend the day on my studies. I don't want to get too far behind. I'll be so glad to get back to work and to school next week.

The shower was refreshing, and after she toweled dry and fluffed her short curls into place, she slipped into a bright, cheerful lounging robe, dabbing on just a touch of makeup and cologne. Then she limped down the stairs and into the kitchen, drawn by the irresistible smell of freshly brewed coffee.

There was a note on the table. She picked it up and read it as she walked over to the cupboard to get a cup.

> Rachel: It appears as if the weather has changed, so I thought I'd better get my shopping done before the rain starts. The coffee's made.—Aunt Mavis.

Rachel dropped an English muffin into the toaster, then reached into the refrigerator for some jam. She was just about to sit down with her coffee when the doorbell rang.

"Just a minute, I'm coming," she called, hobbling into the entryway. She opened the door and caught her breath. "Bill."

"Hello, Rachel."

They stood there, then Bill asked, "May I come in?"

"Oh, well . . . of course. I'm sorry, you just surprised me. I . . . I wasn't expecting you."

Rachel moved back as Bill stepped inside. "No, I don't imagine you were," he answered. "Isn't Aunt Mavis here?"

"No, she's gone shopping." Rachel closed the door, then turned back to Bill. He was standing very close, looking down at her. She'd forgotten how warm and brown his eyes were.

"Jenny told me about your accident. Are you all right?"

"I'm fine." Her eyes felt locked into his. She cleared her throat. "Well, I was just about to have some coffee. Would you . . . care for some?"

"I'd like that very much."

She turned toward the kitchen, with Bill following her.

"You're limping."

"Oh, it's just my ankle, nothing serious. Sit down and I'll get the coffee."

Bill took her arm gently and she looked back at him. "No," he said. "You sit down. I'll get the coffee." He smiled. "I know where everything is around here, remember?"

The concern in his eyes made her weak, and she sank down into the chair. Bill poured his coffee and sat down beside her.

"Aren't you going to eat anything, Rachel? I'll be glad to fix you something."

Rachel remembered the English muffin and looked over at the toaster. "I'd forgotten I fixed a muffin; it's in the toaster." She looked back at Bill. "I'd be glad to . . . share it with you."

Bill smiled, and Rachel had to resist a sudden impulse to reach out and touch the laugh wrinkles around his eyes.

"That would be nice," he answered. "I'll get it. Do we—do you have any jam?"

"Right here." She picked up the jar on the table in front of them. "Raspberry."

"My favorite."

"I know."

He looked at her for a moment longer, then walked over to the toaster and brought the muffin back to the table. He spread the jam on one half and handed it to her. "Almost like old times," he said smiling.

Rachel took the muffin from him, and their hands touched briefly. "Almost," she said softly.

She nibbled at her muffin and sipped her coffee, but she could taste nothing. Oh, God, help me. I don't know how much longer I can hold myself together like this.

"You know, Rachel," Bill said suddenly, setting his coffee down in front of him, "when I heard you'd been in an accident—even though Jenny assured me you were all right—I almost went crazy with worry. I would have come to check on you sooner, but Jenny didn't call me about it until last night. I couldn't sleep after that. All I could think about was you—about all the years we spent together—about how I'd feel if anything ever happened to you. I guess I didn't realize until then how much I still loved you."

The tears came then, and Rachel knew there was no point in trying to stop them. "Oh, Bill, don't," she whispered. "Don't, please."

Bill got up out of his chair and came over to Rachel, kneeling down in front of her. He took her hands in his, and when she looked into his eyes, they were wet with tears, too. Suddenly his pain seemed so much greater than her own, and she pulled one hand away from him and reached out to caress his cheek. He closed his eyes as she traced the lines in his forehead and then laid a finger on his lips. Reaching up and grasping her wrist, he pressed the palm of her hand against his mouth, kissing her gently again and again. "Oh, Rachel," he murmured. "Rachel."

He stood then, pulling her up to face him. Their eyes met as his arms slipped around her waist, pressing her tightly against him until she thought she couldn't breathe. And then he kissed her—softly, but with more passion than Rachel had felt from him in years. If there was a part of her that resisted what she was feeling, it was quickly fading from her consciousness.

Bill kissed her hair, her neck, her ears. "Oh, Rachel," he whispered, "you smell so good. You feel so good." Their lips met again, more urgently this time, and Rachel knew she had yielded herself to him completely.

"Oh, Rachel, I love you so much."

She gasped and shivered as he caressed her. She moaned when she felt the warmth of his lips on her throat. Just when she thought her legs would no longer hold her up, he lifted her in his arms the way he had done so many times when they were first married. His voice was low and husky. "I want to make love to you, Rachel."

She looked up at him as he began to carry her toward the stairs. Oh, my darling, she thought, gazing longingly into his eyes, is this really happening? Are we really going to be together again like before? Before Sheryl and the baby and . . . .

She stiffened. "Oh, Bill," she cried, "what are we doing?" She struggled against him. "Put me down, Bill, please. This is wrong."

Bill frowned as he set her down, his arms still around her. "What do you mean, it's wrong? You're my wife."

She ached to hold him close, to let him carry her to the bedroom, but she couldn't. "I may be your wife, but what about Sheryl—and your baby?" She wondered why her voice sounded so strange, as if she were listening to someone else.

"It was a mistake, Rachel. I know that now. I never should have gotten involved with Sheryl. I never should have left you. I—"

"But you did."

Bill swallowed. "I'm sorry, honey. I'm really sorry. Can't you forgive me?" His eyes were pleading with her as he leaned closer. "Please?"

He kissed her, and suddenly she thought, Yes! Oh, yes, of course I can forgive you, if you'll just come back to me.

He drew back slightly and lifted her chin with his finger. "Please?"

She took a deep breath and nodded. "I forgive you," she whispered. "And I want you to come home. But . . . how will you tell Sheryl?"

He frowned again and his face flushed slightly. "Well, I . . . I don't know. I can't tell her yet. I mean, not right now, not with the baby coming and all." He smiled. "But we can still see each other.

And then, later, after the baby's born, then maybe I can tell her and—"

She pulled away and stared at him in disbelief.

"What's the matter, Rachel?" Bill asked, trying to put his arms around her again. "What's wrong? I don't understand."

She stepped back, pushing his arms away and shaking her head slowly. "You really don't understand, do you?"

"No, Rachel, I don't. I told you I still love you. You said you forgive me. All I want is for you to be patient, give me a little time to—"

"You'd better go, Bill."

"But, Rachel. . . ."

"Please."

He opened his mouth as if to argue, then his jaws clenched and she could see the defeat on his face. His shoulders sagged. "All right. I'll go. But if you ever change your mind. . . ."

Rachel stared into his eyes, feeling as if she were drowning. Or if you ever make up yours, she thought, biting her lip.

"Good-bye, Rachel," Bill said finally, blinking back the tears, then turned and walked out of the kitchen toward the front door. Closing it firmly behind him, he stepped out of the house into the cold gray promise of approaching rain.

* * *

"So, how were things back at the salt mines, Mom?" Chuck joked, as they sat around the dining room table.

"Oh, I was glad to be back," Rachel answered. "The kids made a 'Welcome Back' sign, which they all drew on and signed. It was wonderful. I really missed that place—and, of course, all the kids. And it's good to be back at school, too. I was afraid I might have fallen behind in some of my classes, but I think it's going to be all right. I don't have too much to make up, but I do have quite a bit of homework."

Jennifer giggled, and they all turned to look at her. "Sorry, Mom. I wasn't laughing at you—honest. It's just that I suddenly remembered how many times we've sat around this table talking about my schoolwork, and here I am, listening to my mother talk about hers! Things sure have changed."

They all laughed, including Rachel, but the memory of Bill's visit the previous week cut through her like a knife. Yes, she thought, things certainly have changed.

"Mom?" Rachel heard Chuck's voice calling her. "Mom, can you please pass the salad?"

She shook her head. "Excuse me? Oh, the salad. Of course, honey." She handed him the bowl. "Can I get you anything else?"

"Not yet," he grinned, "but the night is still young." He grimaced. "Oh, what a poor choice of words to use on my thirtieth birthday!"

"Poor baby," Jennifer chuckled, reaching across the table to pat his hand.

"Laugh while you can, little girl," Chuck teased. "Your day will come—and I will show you no mercy."

"Remind me to leave the country when my birthday rolls around," Aunt Mavis said. "If you people think thirty is old, I don't want to be anywhere near this place when you start putting candles on my birthday cake."

Rachel smiled. Thank you, Lord, for my family. What would I ever have done without them? And for my job. You knew how badly I would need it to get through these last few months. It's given me something to look forward to. I need that desperately right now.

"You're as beautiful as ever," Michael had told her. Is that true, Michael? Do you still see something in me of that young woman you met and fell in love with fifteen years ago? There were times, after you left, that I thought the Rachel you knew had disappeared forever. The guilt from our relationship was almost more than I could bear.

And poor Bill. He said I had changed—that I wasn't the same person he had married. I denied it, of course. What else could I do? I was so ashamed. I did everything I could to appear the good and faithful wife—even changed my looks so no other man would ever be interested in me. I suppose I thought I was doing penance somehow.

Oh, Michael, I never meant to hurt you. I never thought you'd come back into my life after all these years. I had almost convinced myself that our affair had never happened—that it was all a bad dream. But it did happen, didn't it, Michael? And Bill was right. I had changed. My guilt changed me; and it drove my husband into the arms of another woman.

"You're not eating, my dear," Aunt Mavis was saying. "Is anything wrong?"

Rachel looked down at her plate and realized she'd been pushing her food around her plate with her fork. "I'm sorry, Aunt Mavis. It's delicious. It's just that . . . well, I'm not very hungry this evening, I'm afraid."

"Hey, no dinner, no birthday cake!" Jennifer exclaimed, grinning widely. "That's the rule, remember? How many times did you make me eat my lima beans before I could have any dessert? Come on, Mom, fair's fair."

Rachel smiled. "I suppose you're right, honey. And it's too good a dinner to waste."

"Oh, nothing's going to go to waste around here," Chuck said, reaching for the mashed potatoes. "After all, my days are numbered now. I've got to eat while I still have some teeth left."

Jennifer shook her head and rolled her eyes. "It's going to catch up with you someday, Chuck Miller. You're going to wake up one morning and weigh three hundred pounds."

"You'll still love me," Chuck grinned, then winked. "For better or worse, remember?"

"Did I say that?" Jennifer asked, raising her eyebrows.

"You sure did!" Chuck answered. "I heard you. In fact, we all heard you, didn't we?" He looked from Rachel to Aunt Mavis.

"I'm afraid so, my dear," Aunt Mavis smiled. "You're stuck with him, Jenny."

"A fate worse than death," Jennifer laughed.

Rachel tried to smile, but her mind had slipped back to her New Year's Eve date with Cal. I had really looked forward to that dinner, she thought. Oh, why do things always seem to begin with such promise, and then end with so much heartache? I was foolish to jump into that relationship with Cal so quickly, but I had hoped.... She sighed. You used to tell me how beautiful I was, too, didn't you, Cal? And the last time we talked you were so sure you were in love with me. Are you, Cal? Are you really? Michael says he is. And now Bill insists he is, too. For someone who supposedly has three men in love with her, I seem to be doing an awful lot of crying.

"Well, let's clear the table," Aunt Mavis said, standing up. "It's time for cake and ice cream. Chuck, you sit still—it's your birthday. You don't have to help."

"Thanks, Aunt Mavis. It's tough getting up at my age, anyway."

Aunt Mavis chuckled as she gathered the plates together.

"I'll light the candles," Jennifer offered. She turned to look at Chuck, her eyes twinkling mischievously. "Of course, it may take awhile."

Chuck laughed and threw his napkin at her as she scampered into the kitchen.

"You two have such a good marriage," Rachel smiled. "Don't ever let anything happen to ruin it, Chuck."

His smile faded and he looked at Rachel. "I won't," he promised. "Not ever."

Rachel stood up and carried the remaining dishes into the kitchen.

"Shall we have our cake in the dining room or move into the den?" Aunt Mavis asked.

"Oh, let's go into the den," Jennifer said. "It's so much more comfortable—and less formal."

Rachel smiled at her daughter. "Good idea. We can start a fire in the fireplace and sit around and get fat."

Jennifer laughed. "Oh, yes, let's. In fact, there are enough candles right here on this birthday cake to get the fireplace roaring."

"I heard that," Chuck called out.

They laughed as they picked up the cake and walked into the dining room singing "Happy Birthday."

* * *

As Rachel drove home from work two days later, she smiled as the sun peeked through the clouds. *It's going to turn into a nice day, after all. I think I'll do some swimming before lunch, and then work out in the garden for a while before I tackle the rest of that assignment for class tomorrow.*

She stopped at a red light. *I suppose that's as good a plan as any,* she thought wryly. *Just stay busy, Rachel, old girl. Fill up your days so you don't have time to think about the past—or too far into the future. That way you can't dwell on what you've lost—or what you may never have again.*

The light turned green and she pressed the accelerator. *Am I wrong not to hang on anymore? Should I fight for Bill? Or maybe I should take Michael up on his offer to take care of me. He was always so good to me. Maybe I would learn to love him in time. Maybe it would be better than spending the rest of my life alone.*

Pulling into her driveway, she pushed the automatic door opener and drove into the garage. *Oh, God, I know it's time for me to let go of the past and go on with my life, but I don't know if I can. And I'm not sure which direction to take. How do I let go, Lord? How much do I let go? Do I try to forget about Bill, or hope that everything will work out someday? And what about Michael? And Cal? Is he really a part of my past? Or is he a part of my future that I never gave a chance?*

She opened the back door from the garage to the kitchen and walked in.

"Well, there you are!" Aunt Mavis exclaimed, looking up from the stove. "I thought you'd never get home."

Rachel frowned. "Am I late? Did I forget something?"

Aunt Mavis turned and wiped her hands on the dish towel. "No, you're not late. And you didn't forget anything." She walked over to the table and picked up a white box. "This came for you today. It's from the florist—the same one that brought that bouquet of gardenias on Valentine's Day." She raised her eyebrows. "I don't suppose you're going to tell me who they're from?"

Rachel didn't answer. She walked over to her aunt and took the box. She stared at it for a moment, then looked up. "Excuse me, Aunt Mavis. I believe I'll open this in my room."

Aunt Mavis shrugged. "Why not? Why should anybody tell me what's going on around here? What business is it of mine, anyway?"

"I'm sorry. It's just—"

"Forget it," Aunt Mavis interrupted with a smile. "I'm only teasing you. Go on. Go into your room and open it."

Rachel went up to her room and closed the door. She sat down on her bed, her hands trembling, and carefully opened the box. She knew from the fragrance even before she saw it that the single gardenia was from Michael. And she knew there would be no card, because she knew what he was telling her.

She sat there, staring at the gardenia, but she did not lift it out of its box. "Good-bye, Michael," she said finally, then stood up and walked over to the small wastepaper basket in the corner. She dropped the box into the basket, then took a deep breath and went over to the phone by her bed. Shaking, she dialed the number.

"Langsford and Jordan. May I help you?"

"Sylvia? This is Rachel Webster. Is Cal—Mr. Langsford—free? I need to speak with him for a moment, if I may."

"Why, yes, Mrs. Webster, as a matter of fact, he is. Just a minute. I'll connect you."

Rachel chewed a fingernail nervously while she waited for Cal to pick up the phone.

"Rachel? Is that you?"

"Yes, Cal, it is." She swallowed. "How are you?"

She could almost see him smiling as he answered. "Better than I've been in a long time, thanks to your call. What can I do for you?"

"I . . . I'd like to see you, if I could. I know I should have made the appointment with Sylvia, but. . . ."

"Don't be silly. When and where? You name it."

"How about if I come to your office tomorrow after my class? About noon?"

"That's perfect. Maybe . . . we could have lunch?"

"Maybe. I'll see you then, Cal."

Chapter 19

As Rachel stepped into the office, the sliding glass window opened and Sylvia poked her head out. "Hi there," she called cheerily. "You're right on time."

Rachel returned Sylvia's smile. "It's good to see you again, Sylvia. How are you?"

"I'm fine, thanks. You look great."

"Thank you. Is Mr. Langsford ready for me yet?"

Sylvia lowered her voice and leaned forward. "He certainly is. He's been running around here for the past hour making sure that he was caught up and didn't have any other clients left to see before you arrived." She glanced around the empty office and winked at Rachel. "I think you've got him all to yourself."

Rachel could feel her face growing hot, as Sylvia got up and came around to open the door to the inner offices. "Just go in," she whispered. "I'll hold all his calls."

Walking down the hall to Cal's office, Rachel took a deep breath and squared her shoulders. Her hand shook slightly as she knocked on the heavy wooden door. There was no answer. She was about to knock again when the door swung open.

Cal's grin spread across his face and his gray eyes sparkled. "Come in, Rachel," he said softly. "Please."

Rachel walked past him as he stepped back; then she turned to him and cleared her throat. "I thought it was time for us to talk."

Cal closed the door and moved toward her. "I'm glad, Rachel. We left so many things unsaid. I've been hoping for a chance like this." He pointed to the sofa beside the wall. "Can we sit over there? It seems so formal staring at each other across my desk."

Rachel nodded. "Of course."

She sat down on one end of the couch. Cal seated himself next to her, but with enough distance between them that they weren't touching. For a moment, neither of them spoke.

"Well," Cal said, "where do we start?"

"I'm not sure. It seemed I had so much to say to you before I got here. Now, I . . . ."

"I know what you mean. I've rehearsed this in my mind a hundred times. I didn't sleep last night, thinking about how our meeting might turn out." He hesitated. "I've missed you, Rachel. So very much."

Rachel looked down at her hands folded in her lap. Maybe I've made a mistake in coming here, she thought. Maybe I should have left well enough alone.

"Rachel?"

She looked back up. He was staring at her, his eyes wide and expectant. She remembered how vulnerable he had seemed the day she had sat across from him at the deli, poking at his potato salad with his fork while he told her how his marriage had ended when Edith left him. That was the first time I thought of you as more than my lawyer, Cal. You were someone who could understand my pain, because you had been through it, too.

"Rachel, what is it? What are you thinking? What's going on in your life?"

She cleared her throat again. "Well, I . . . ." She took another deep breath. "Well, first of all, I want to discuss the settlement."

The light in Cal's eyes faded. "Oh, well, you know what I've always told you about that. It's more than likely going to hold up everything because I think you're asking for too much. As I've told you before, Rachel, your demands are unreasonable."

"I agree."

Cal raised his eyebrows. "You do? What brought this on?"

Rachel shrugged. "I've been doing a lot of thinking, Cal. And you're right. I am being unreasonable. Bill is willing to give me the

193

house, which, as you already pointed out to me, is paid for. He is also willing to give me a comfortable monthly income. And I do have a substantial amount in the bank that my parents left me. I don't need the business, too."

Cal shook his head. "You're full of surprises, aren't you? Well, this will certainly make things easier all the way around. With this concession on your part, I don't see any problems with the divorce going through on schedule."

Rachel swallowed the lump in her throat, but said nothing..

Cal smiled. "I'm pleased with your decision, Rachel—personally, as well as professionally. You know, Edith and I are getting a divorce, too. We both agreed it's for the best—under the circumstances."

She scanned his face. "What *are* the circumstances, Cal?"

"Well, number one, of course, is that Edith still says she isn't ready to come home. And . . . number two . . . I told her I'm in love with you. I also told her I hope to convince you to marry me someday."

"I see."

"Am I . . . out of line to think that, Rachel? I mean, do I have a chance? Do you think that maybe . . . someday?"

Dear Lord, help me with this. She took a deep, shaky breath. "No, Cal. I don't think so. I'm sorry, but as I said, I've been doing a lot of thinking. And I've realized some things about myself that I wasn't aware of before. I know now that when our relationship began, I was lonely—and very vulnerable. I wasn't thinking clearly, Cal. You were warm and wonderful. You made me feel wanted and beautiful. Do you know how long it had been since I'd felt that way? I needed you. And I'm ashamed to admit, I used you. Not intentionally, of course. I had no idea what I was doing. I truly believed at the time that we might have a future together. I know better now."

The pain in his eyes cut her deeply, and she reached out to cover his hand with her own. "I'm so sorry. I never meant to hurt you. And I know you didn't mean to hurt me. But we did hurt each other, didn't we? We were two very lonely people, using each other for comfort."

"But I love you, Rachel," Cal whispered hoarsely. "I truly do."

"Maybe so. I don't know. But, you see, I . . . I realized something else about myself, Cal. I realized that the only man I have ever loved is my husband. I know he won't be my husband legally much longer, but I still love him. And I would give anything in the world if I could have him back. In fact, I seriously considered dropping the divorce altogether, but I think maybe it's best to let it go all the way up to the signing of the final papers, then force Bill to decide what it is he truly wants to do. He can't rebuild a life with me or a new life with Sheryl until he makes a choice, once and for all. Either way, I must go on."

"Let me help you, Rachel. Let me help you get over him. I love you so much. Just give me a chance to prove that to you. I'll help you forget him."

Rachel shook her head. "No, Cal. No. You must understand. Although Bill is involved with someone else right now, he's still the man I love. I don't know if I'll ever get over that. But I do know that I must go on with my life. And the only way for me to do that is to learn to cope without him." Her voice cracked. "I don't want a substitute, Cal, and I'm afraid that's what you'd be. It wouldn't be fair to you."

Cal sighed deeply. "I suppose not. Although at this point, I feel as if I'd take you under any conditions—even if I knew you didn't feel the same about me as I do toward you."

"You might feel that way now, but you wouldn't for long. You deserve much more."

His eyes glistened with tears as Rachel squeezed his hand. "I'd better go," she said softly. He was still sitting there when she got up and quietly let herself out of his office.

* * *

"Whew! It's been a long morning."

Rachel laughed. "It certainly has. Is it just my imagination,

Susan, or are these kids more wound up today than usual?"

"It's not your imagination, I guarantee you. What do you suppose it is, spring fever? They're wild."

"Well, at least we're in the homestretch—it's almost noon. I pity the afternoon crew trying to get these wiggly worms down for their naps."

"Miss Rachel, Miss Rachel."

Rachel looked down as she felt a tug on her apron. Jeremy's upturned face was flushed and dirty and his hair hung damp against his forehead. "Miss Rachel, watch how fast I can run."

Before Rachel could answer, Jeremy had taken off across the playground, charging past the swings and sandbox toward the chain link fence. He bounced off the fence and turned back, bumping into Christopher, who had apparently seen him running and decided to join in the fun. They both landed in a heap as Rachel and Susan hurried over to them.

"Are you two all right?" Susan asked, bending down beside Christopher.

Christopher looked up and grinned impishly as he rubbed his dark, bouncy curls. "I fell down."

"Me, too," Jeremy chimed in. "Did you see me run, Miss Rachel?"

Rachel swallowed a grin and tried to look serious. "I certainly did, Jeremy. And you were very fast. But do we have a rule here at our school about running?"

Rachel and Susan looked from Jeremy to Christopher. The boys' eyes were big, but neither answered.

"I believe the rule is no running on the playground except in the grassy area over there," Susan said, pointing to the opposite end of the playground. "Do you two understand now why we have that rule?"

Christopher and Jeremy exchanged sheepish glances.

"We have that rule," Rachel explained, "so things like this won't happen. We don't want anyone getting hurt around here, do we?"

Christopher shook his head and looked down.

"I forgot," Jeremy answered, his lower lip quivering.

"Well, no one was hurt this time, but just so you won't forget again, why don't you both take a time-out?" Rachel indicated the bench beside the sandbox. "You two sit down there on the bench quietly for a few minutes and think about the rule so next time you'll remember, okay?"

The boys nodded, and Jeremy hung his head as they walked slowly toward the bench. Rachel and Susan smiled and winked at each other.

After about five minutes Rachel walked over to the boys. Christopher was already gazing longingly at the playground, his eyes shining, when he noticed Rachel approaching.

"Can I go now, Miss Rachel?" he asked.

"Have you thought about what we talked about, Christopher?"

"Yes, and I won't run, I promise."

"All right," Rachel smiled. "You go on and play then."

Christopher jumped off the bench and started to run, then turned and looked at Rachel and grinned as he backed slowly away. The minute his feet touched the grass he was running as fast as his short little legs could carry him.

Like a bird let out of its cage, Rachel thought, smiling to herself and sitting down next to Jeremy. "How about you, Jeremy? Are you ready to go play?"

Jeremy didn't look up.

"Aren't you going to talk to me?" Rachel asked. "Are you mad at me, Jeremy?"

Jeremy shook his head.

"Do you want to talk about it?"

He shook his head again.

Rachel sighed loudly. "Well, all right. But it certainly makes me feel bad when you won't talk to me. I thought we were friends."

"We are," Jeremy answered in a tiny voice.

"Then why don't you look at me, Jeremy, and tell me what's wrong?"

Jeremy raised his head slowly. There were tear stains on his dirty cheeks. "I'm sorry, Miss Rachel."

Rachel put an arm around his shoulder. "I know you are, Jeremy. And I know you just forgot about the rule. I'll bet you'll try really hard to remember it from now on, won't you?"

Jeremy nodded.

"Hi, Jeremy," a voice called from behind them.

They both turned. Jeremy's mother stood at the entrance to the playground.

"Mommy!" Jeremy jumped up and began to run toward the gate, then stopped and walked slowly with Rachel following behind.

"I'm walking because we're only supposed to run on the grass," Jeremy announced to his mother as he stopped in front of the gate.

"That sounds like a very good idea," Jeremy's mother smiled, opening the gate and reaching down to pick up her son. "How are you?" she asked, turning toward Rachel.

"Fine, Mrs. Decker. How are you?"

"Julia, remember? And I'm fine, too."

"You're here early today."

"Yes, I got the afternoon off and thought I'd come pick up Jeremy and take him out to lunch."

Jeremy's eyes lit up. "Oh, goody! Can we get a hot dog with ketchup?"

Julia laughed. "Of course we can."

"Can Miss Rachel come, too?"

Rachel smiled. "Oh, thank you, Jeremy. I'd love to, but I have to get home and do some studying, I'm afraid."

Jeremy turned to his mother. "Miss Rachel goes to school, just like me and Carrie!"

"Well, good for her," Julia answered, then looked back at Rachel. "By the way, there is something I wanted to talk to you about, if you have a minute."

"Sure, what is it?"

"Well, as you know, Jeremy is absolutely crazy about that little lamb you bought him. And . . . well, he's been after Mark and me to come to church sometime. He keeps saying he wants to go to 'Miss Rachel's church.' You're turning him into quite a persistent missionary, I'm afraid."

"Oh, I'm sorry," Rachel apologized. "I certainly didn't mean to cause any problems for you. We've just talked about . . . Jesus . . . a few times. Jeremy is so curious."

"It's all right. I understand. And, believe me, I don't mind a bit. In fact, Mark has finally agreed that we should all start going to church—as a family. I'm just thrilled. I've wanted this for so long. But we're a little hesitant about walking into a new church for the first time. I wonder if . . . well, would it be an imposition if we . . . could we sit with you in church this Sunday? Just until we get used to things. Would that be all right?"

"Oh, well, I . . . ."

"If it's a problem . . ."

"No, of course not. I'd love to have you . . . join us . . . on Sunday. Is the early service all right?"

I just hope the church roof doesn't fall in, Rachel thought. Except for the Christmas pageant, I haven't been there in six months. Oh, well, at least Aunt Mavis will be happy.

* * *

Jeremy wriggled excitedly on the pew between Rachel and his mother. His sister, Carrie, sat between her parents, while Aunt Mavis, wearing a new dress and a big smile, had parked herself on Rachel's right. When Rachel had announced her plans to attend church that Sunday ("Just to help Jeremy and his family get settled in"), Aunt Mavis had been thrilled.

She's been beaming like a neon light ever since, Rachel thought.

"We take up almost the whole pew, huh, Miss Rachel?" Jeremy whispered loudly.

Rachel smiled and nodded.

"Why do they call it a 'pew'?" Jeremy asked.

"Shhh," Julia warned, placing her hand on Jeremy's arm. Then she looked over at Rachel and smiled.

What a lovely family, Rachel sighed. I just pray nothing ever happens to drive them apart.

She glanced down at Jeremy. He looked so grown up in his jacket and bow tie, although he had complained to Rachel that he didn't like his tie. "I want a long one—like Daddy's."

She looked over at Jeremy's father. Even sitting down Mark seemed tall, especially next to his petite wife. Rachel couldn't see Carrie's face without leaning forward, but she could see her thin legs swinging back and forth, until Mark put his hand on Carrie's knee. He didn't say anything, but Carrie sat very still after that.

As the choir began to sing, Jeremy stopped his wiggling. His brown eyes were open wide and he stared straight ahead. Rachel looked away from him to Aunt Mavis. She was staring straight ahead, too, but she was still wearing her smile.

Rachel was thankful they had taken up almost an entire pew. She really wasn't anxious to have anyone come and sit down beside her and start asking her where she'd been, or commenting on how glad they all were to see her back. She just wanted to sit there until the service was over, and then slip out quietly, un-noticed. She knew, however, how impossible that would be with Aunt Mavis around. No doubt her aunt would want to introduce the Deckers to everyone in the building. And, of course, she'd al-ready mentioned to Rachel that they should stay after church ser-vice for Sunday school so Jeremy and Carrie could get started in their classes. "And you can take Mark and Julia down to that young couples' class," she had said, as they pulled up in front of the church. "I'm sure they'd enjoy it. Then you can come to class with me. We're doing a wonderful study right now on the book of Hebrews. It follows right along with Pastor Mitch's Sunday morn-ing messages."

Rachel hadn't answered, but she knew she was stuck—at least for today. I'm sorry, Lord, it's nothing personal. It's just that . . .

well, I'm not ready for this yet. I can't stand the thought of facing everyone, of their questions or—even worse—their pity. Oh, just help me get through this and get me out of here.

Her mind drifted back to the last time she had sat here in this church—the "Christmas package," as Jeremy still called it. What an adorable little shepherd you were, she thought, glancing over at him. It's hard to believe that was only three months ago. So much has happened since then.

She felt her cheeks grow hot as she remembered leaving the pageant with Cal, the drive to his apartment, the way he'd held her and kissed her and. . . . Oh, God, I knew what was going to happen, even before we got out of the car and climbed the stairs to his front door. I'm so sorry, Lord.

And then she thought of Michael. Dear, dear Michael. I never meant to hurt you, either. I still have a hard time accepting the fact that our affair really happened. I tried so desperately to forget it.

Tears came to her eyes as she thought then of Bill. You're the one I've hurt the most, my darling. And you don't even know it. You still think that you're the one who broke up our marriage. I wish I could take that guilt away from you by telling you about Michael, but what good would it do now? It would only hurt you more. Maybe someday I'll be able to tell you. Maybe some-day. . . .

Oh, Lord, I've made such a mess of things. Can you ever truly forgive me?

Suddenly the pastor's words broke through and she was shocked to realize he was already preaching. I haven't been paying any attention to the service at all, she thought guiltily. She glanced at her watch. My goodness, he's almost through. And I haven't heard a thing he's said. She stared at him, trying to concentrate. She gasped when she heard his next words.

"Some of you are sitting out there thinking you've committed the worst sins on earth, that God couldn't possibly forgive you. That's a lie," he exclaimed, "and don't you believe it for one more minute. Look at that verse again—Hebrews, chapter thirteen, verse eight: 'Jesus Christ is the same yesterday and today and forever.'" He turned and pointed above the altar. "How many times have you seen that verse right here above this altar? How many times have you read it without thinking about how powerful a verse it really is?"

He turned back toward the congregation and looked in Rachel's direction. She was sure he had meant those words just for her. Did Aunt Mavis tell him I was coming this morning? Is that why he's saying the same things to me that she said the day I came home from the hospital? Did they plan this?

But the gentle tugging at her heart assured her that, although Pastor Mitch and Aunt Mavis were definitely being used in this plan, it had not originated with them. She could hold back the tears no longer, and when the pastor asked for those to come to the altar who wanted to give their hearts and lives over to this one who alone never changes, Rachel thought suddenly of the story of the wayward prodigal son returning to his father, and she knew it was time to come home.

As she hurried down the aisle to the altar, tears streaming down her face, she wasn't even aware that Mark and Julia were walking down the aisle, hand in hand, behind her.

Chapter 20

Rachel drove home from school the next day, sure that the sun was somehow brighter, the sky bluer. She pushed the electric window button and took a deep breath as the breeze ruffled her hair. *It's a beautiful day, Lord. Thank you, thank you.*

She pulled into her driveway and stopped. Jennifer's car was parked in front of the garage. Rachel switched off the ignition and jumped out of the car. *What a wonderful surprise,* she thought.

"I'm home," she called, hurrying into the house, but there was no answer. She set her purse down on the table in the entryway and walked down the hall toward the den. "Hello?"

"Out here," Jennifer's voice called from the patio. "We're sitting outside enjoying the gorgeous weather."

Rachel opened the screen on the sliding glass door and walked outside. "Don't get up," she said, bending over to kiss Jennifer and then Aunt Mavis. "I'll just get a chair and join you. You're right, it is a gorgeous day."

She pulled up a chair beside her daughter. "And to what do we owe this delightful surprise?"

Jennifer shrugged, but her eyes sparkled mischievously. "Oh, no special reason." She glanced at Aunt Mavis and winked.

"Well," Aunt Mavis said, standing up, "I'm certainly glad you're home, my dear. I believe I'll leave you here to entertain Jenny while I go fix us some lunch."

After she was gone, Rachel looked at Jennifer. "All right, what's going on here? I saw that wink—and I'd know that 'cat-that-swallowed-the-canary' look of yours anywhere. What gives?"

Jennifer grinned. "Well, actually, Aunt Mavis called us last night. She told us you went to church yesterday."

Rachel raised her eyebrows. "Oh, she did, did she?" She smiled. "Can't a person have any secrets around this place?"

"Not from the people who love you."

Rachel laughed. "Then I suppose she told you the rest—that I went forward when Pastor Mitch gave the altar call?"

Jennifer nodded. "Yes. Oh, Mom, I'm so glad. I just know everything's going to be all right now. I know it."

"You're right, darling. I know it, too. Although I really don't know anymore now about what the future holds than I did before. But it's good to trust God again—to know that I'm back on the right track." She reached over and took Jennifer's hand and squeezed it.

Jennifer sighed. "I only wish Daddy would come around. It must be so hard on him, going through life trying to handle everything on his own. If only he could let go and realize how much Jesus loves him."

"I know, honey. I'm praying that he turns his life over to Jesus, too. But, you know what? I realized yesterday how very patient God has been with me, how much he's loved me all along, even when I wasn't sure he was there anymore. Do you think he'll do any less for your father? Just keep praying. It's going to be all right, Jenny."

"You're right, Mom. It's just that . . . oh, Mom, if only they weren't expecting a baby. How can things ever work out now?"

Rachel shook her head. "I don't have an answer for you, honey. How I wish I did! But we just have to believe that God does, right?"

Jennifer nodded again.

"Jenny, there's something else we need to talk about."

"What's that, Mom?"

Rachel hesitated. "Sheryl—and the baby."

Jennifer's chin came up and her eyes narrowed slightly. "What about them?"

"You've got to accept the fact that your father and Sheryl are living together right now, and that they're going to have a baby very soon."

Jennifer let go of her mother's hand. "I don't know if I can, Mom. How can I accept Dad's relationship with Sheryl? I mean, she's the reason you and Dad aren't together anymore."

Rachel flinched, thinking of Michael. "I know it won't be easy, honey. But you have to try. Your father needs you right now."

"That's what he keeps telling me, Mom. But if he needs me so badly, why did he leave us for a new family? Why does he want to start over now? Why couldn't he have been satisfied with you and me? And how am I ever going to accept the fact that my own father had an affair?"

Should I tell her about Michael? Rachel wondered. No, I can't. I just can't. It would be too much for her to handle. Rachel took a deep breath and tried to hold her voice steady. "Honey, as you get older, you'll realize that people sometimes do things without thinking about the consequences. I believe that's what has happened with your father. But, whatever the reason, what's happened has happened, and we can't turn back the clock. All we can do now is go on from here. You've got to maintain your relationship with your father, Jenny. You've got to."

"I suppose you're right."

"And, Jenny, you've got to think of that baby, too."

Jennifer's dark eyes flashed for a split second. "What do you mean by that?"

"I mean that none of this is that little baby's fault. He or she is going to be arriving in this world under some pretty tough circumstances. Since you'll be the big sister, I hope you give that baby all the love and help you can manage."

Jennifer sat silently for a moment. "You're right, Mom," she answered finally. "But it's so hard."

"I know it is, honey. I know it is. But you have to try."

"I will. I promise."

Rachel smiled. "Of course you will. You're a wonderful

daughter. I don't know what I'd do without you."

Jennifer smiled back. "Well, you'll never have to worry about that." She paused. "As a matter of fact, Mom, I came up here today for two reasons. One, of course, was to tell you how happy I was about yesterday—about church and all. But I had another reason, too."

"Oh, really? What?"

"I saw the doctor last week. He said Chuck and I can start planning our family again. He said I can get pregnant, Mom."

Rachel felt a chill pass over her in spite of the warm spring sunshine. "Oh, Jenny, I'm happy for you. But, are you sure? Are you sure you're up to it? The doctor doesn't think there'll be any problems?"

"He said he sees no reason why I can't have a normal pregnancy. He wants me to take care of myself and come to see him as soon as I suspect anything, but, otherwise, he says not to worry."

"Well, you listen to him," Rachel warned. "You take good care of yourself. Eat right, get plenty of rest, and—"

Jennifer laughed. "Oh, Mom, I know all that. Besides, do you think I'd have a chance of doing anything less with Chuck around? He hovers over me like a mother hen as it is. Sometimes I think he's afraid I'm going to break or something."

"It's because he loves you so much, honey."

"I know that. I'm not complaining, believe me. Chuck is a wonderful husband—and I know he'll be a great father someday. But the point is, you don't need to worry about me."

"You're right, of course. Have you told Aunt Mavis yet?"

"No, I was waiting for you. Shall we go tell her now?"

Rachel stood up and pulled Jennifer to her feet. "By all means. Let's go tell her."

* * *

When Rachel's alarm went off two days later, she shut it off and squinted at it. How come six o'clock always comes so early?

206

She stretched and yawned. Oh, what I wouldn't give to roll over and go back to sleep. No, can't do it—I have two classes this morning. Okay, up and at 'em, old girl.

By the time she got out of the shower she was wide awake. Opening her bedroom door and stepping out into the hallway, she could already smell the coffee. Mmm, nobody makes coffee like Aunt Mavis. But I'm surprised she's up so early this morning. She didn't get home from her meeting until late last night.

"Good morning, dear," Aunt Mavis greeted her, as she walked into the kitchen. "I was just making some whole wheat pancakes. How many would you like?"

"Oh, just one, Aunt Mavis, please. I'm not very hungry this morning."

Aunt Mavis raised an eyebrow disapprovingly, but didn't say anything. She flipped the pancakes over in the pan and poured some coffee into the mugs.

Rachel sat down. "You know," she commented as Aunt Mavis carried the plates of pancakes over to the table, "I've been thinking. The college will be closed for a week next month—during Easter, you know—and so will the preschool. I wonder if that offer from Chuck's parents is still good?"

Aunt Mavis sat down next to her. "What offer is that, my dear?"

"Oh, you remember, when Chuck and Jenny got back from their trip to Colorado they said that Chuck's parents would like to have me come back and visit them sometime. I think I just might do that during Easter vacation."

"Why, Rachel, that's a wonderful idea. The change of scenery would do you a world of good."

Rachel nodded. "That's what I was thinking." She passed the syrup to Aunt Mavis. "Besides, I haven't flown anywhere in a long time. Would you take me to the airport?"

"Of course I would." She chuckled. "With bells on."

Rachel smiled. "Your enthusiasm is good for me, Aunt Mavis. I don't know what I would do without you."

"Oh, I think you'd do just fine, my dear. Really."

Rachel shook her head. "I don't know. I've gotten so used to having you around."

Aunt Mavis didn't answer.

"I've been thinking about something else, Aunt Mavis."

Aunt Mavis raised her eyebrows. "My goodness, you've certainly been busy thinking lately, haven't you?"

Rachel grinned. "Yes, I have. I've been thinking about how much I dislike this house. You know, I never did want to move in here. I only went along with it because of Bill." She stopped and swallowed, then took a deep breath. "I'm thinking about selling it."

Aunt Mavis laid down her fork. "That's a big decision, Rachel."

"I know. But I'm getting better at making decisions lately. Besides, not only do I hate this house, I hate this furniture. It's just not me, Aunt Mavis. I started thinking how nice it would be to find a smaller place somewhere—an apartment, maybe. You know, one where I would still have access to a swimming pool, but where I wouldn't feel as though I were rattling around in some mausoleum or something."

"I'd hardly call this house a mausoleum, dear. Still, I can certainly understand your feelings."

"I could get a smaller place, and then get all of Grandma and Grandpa's antiques down from the attic again. I always loved those antiques. They're me, Aunt Mavis. This place and this modern furniture just aren't. They never have been. And, since I have to face the fact that Bill may never again be a part of my life, well . . . I have to make plans to go on, with or without him. If things do somehow work out someday and we get back together again, I'd rather start over in a new place—one without so many bad memories."

Aunt Mavis nodded. "You're right, my dear. And I tell you what. If you do decide to sell this place, I'll help you look for a new one."

"Thanks. I may take you up on that. But I don't want you to

think that I'm doing this to get rid of you. I mean, I haven't really decided yet. And if I do, it will probably be months before the house sells, and—"

Aunt Mavis put her hand on Rachel's arm. "Don't worry about me. As a matter of fact, the reason I'm up so early this morning is that I was going to go over to my apartment and open things up and air it out a bit. To tell you the truth, I've been trying to think of some way to tell you that I think it's time for me to move back home."

"Oh, Aunt Mavis, no. I don't want you to go. That's not why I mentioned selling the house, really. Oh, I'll admit, I wasn't too thrilled when you first showed up here and announced that you were moving in, but now I can't imagine life without you."

Aunt Mavis laughed. "Oh, Rachel, it's not as if I'd be moving to Siberia, you know. I'm only going across town. It's just that, well, I think I've been here long enough. I came here to take care of you. I think you can do that for yourself now."

"Oh, Aunt Mavis, I don't know. . . ."

"Well, I do. I know you have a long, hard road ahead of you, my dear. But I also know that you're going to be all right. I must admit, I wasn't too sure there for a while, but now there's no doubt in my mind."

Rachel looked at her aunt affectionately and blinked back a tear, then reached out and touched her cheek. "I'm so glad you came to stay with me, Aunt Mavis."

Aunt Mavis smiled and her blue eyes twinkled. "I know, my dear. I know."

* * *

Rachel got out of her car and let herself into the kitchen from the garage. Well, that finishes my classes for this week. It's been a long day. Tomorrow's Saturday. I think I'll sleep in and then spend the entire day swimming and working in the yard. This weather is absolutely wonderful.

She walked into the den and plopped down on the couch,

kicking off her shoes. *I wonder where Aunt Mavis is? I didn't see her car. Maybe she'd like to go out for dinner tonight. We haven't done that in a while.*

She looked over at the fireplace. *Snuffy. I still miss you so terribly. I keep expecting to look over and see you lying there. It's so hard to believe I didn't want you when Bill first brought you home. And even harder to believe that you're gone.*

She sighed. *How true it is, Lord—what Aunt Mavis and Pastor Mitch said—that you're the only one who never changes. Everything else in my life seems to have been turned upside down in the last six months. But at least I know now that I can always count on you. It certainly took me a long time to figure that out, didn't it? Thank you for being so patient.*

Oh, God, it's so hard to accept all of this. She closed her eyes and thought of the house she had lived in with Bill when they were first married. *We were so happy then, weren't we, darling? If anyone had told us we would end up like this, we would never have believed them. We thought our love was bulletproof, that we were invincible! But then, the very young always do, don't they?*

Do you remember the day we brought Jenny home from the hospital? We thought we had everything we could ever want. I used to watch you with her—you looked so much alike! And you were so proud. I know you never meant to get too busy for her—or for me. You just wanted so much to make the business successful, to give us all the things you thought you should as a husband and a father. I should have been more understanding. I should have stood by you and been more supportive, taken more of an interest in the business.

She opened her eyes and stood up. *But I didn't, and I've got to stop blaming myself for that. And for what happened with Michael and Cal, too. It's not easy, Lord, but if you can forgive me, then I must forgive myself—and go on with my life.*

"Well, there you are, my dear. I didn't hear you come in."

Rachel spun around. "Aunt Mavis! You startled me. I didn't realize you were home. I didn't see your car."

"I left it down at the station for a tune-up, and then took a bus home." She paused. "I've been up in my room—packing some things."

"Oh."

"I haven't had a chance to do anything about dinner yet. Are you hungry?"

"Actually, I was just thinking how nice it would be if you and I went out for dinner tonight. What do you think?"

"Why, Rachel, that's a lovely idea. What time do you want to go?"

"Oh, not for a little while. Do you mind waiting?"

"Not at all. I'm really not that hungry yet."

Rachel walked over and opened the sliding glass door. "I believe I'll go sit out on the patio. Care to join me?"

"Sure. Why not? I love sitting outside in the afternoons this time of year. You know, tomorrow's the first day of spring. I always look forward to the days getting longer and warmer."

Stepping outside, they pulled two chairs over into the late afternoon sun, then closed their eyes and sat silently, basking in the warmth and enjoying the quiet. "I really should go in and shower and change before we go out," Rachel murmured, "but it feels so good out here."

"It does, doesn't it? Let's just sit and enjoy it. There's no rush. We're grown-ups, remember? We can do anything we like."

Rachel looked over at her aunt and laughed. "You're wonderful, Aunt Mavis."

Aunt Mavis smiled, but did not open her eyes. "Yes, I suppose I am."

Rachel leaned back in her chair. "Things could be a lot worse, couldn't they?"

"They certainly could, my dear. They certainly could. In fact," she added, looking over at Rachel, "I'd say they were—not too very long ago, either."

Rachel swallowed. "You're right. I was so hurt, Aunt Mavis, and so confused. I didn't know what to do. I wanted to go to

211

sleep and never wake up. Or better yet, to wake up and find out it was all just a bad dream; to wake up and see Bill lying there beside me. Oh, Aunt Mavis," she moaned, "I still miss him so much."

"I know you do, Rachel. And I wish I could tell you it would all work out someday for you and Bill, or that the pain would go away with time, but I don't know if it will or not. Oh, it will get easier, I suppose, but go away? I don't know."

"I just wish I knew what lay ahead, Aunt Mavis. It's scary sometimes, not knowing."

"None of us knows what's going to happen five minutes from now, Rachel, no matter what our situation might be. But, sometimes, when everything seems to be going our way, we get lulled into a false sense of security. We forget that what we have today could be gone tomorrow. That's why it's so important to have your faith centered on the one who loved you enough to die for you—and whose love never changes. As long as he knows what the future holds, you can relax and trust him to see you through—whatever tomorrow might bring."

"It does make all the difference, doesn't it? I still hurt, I still miss Bill, I still get lonely and scared and depressed—but it's different somehow. When I concentrate on Jesus, I know I'm going to make it."

"You bet you are."

"Even after you move back home?"

"You'll never even notice I'm gone."

Rachel smiled. "Why is it I find that more than just a little hard to believe?"

The breeze started up then, and Rachel sniffed the air. "Oh, Aunt Mavis, orange blossoms. Do you smell them?"

"Mmm, yes, I do."

Rachel closed her eyes, letting the breeze toss her hair and breathing in the sweet, heady fragrance of the orange blossoms. "I love spring, Aunt Mavis," she sighed. "It holds such promise."

The Author

Kathi Mills is an award-winning writer whose credits include a weekly newspaper column, short stories for both children and adults, poems, and numerous magazine articles. Her first book, *A Moment a Day: Practical Devotions for Today's Busy Woman* (co-compiled with Mary Beckwith), was released by Regal Books in 1988. A contributor to Standard Publishing's children's anthology *God Is Everywhere,* Kathi has completed a collection of short stories for Standard, scheduled for release in July 1989. Her nonfiction book, *Broken to Bless,* is also scheduled for 1989 release by Regal Books, and Kathi is now busy working on her second novel, *My Son, John.*

Recently nominated to the *World's Who's Who of Writers and Authors,* Kathi writes, edits, and ghostwrites for several publishers. A creative writing teacher, Kathi is a frequent speaker and leader at writing seminars. She is also a professional member of the National Writers Club and the National League of American Pen Women.

A native Californian, Kathi studied Advanced News Editing at USC. The mother of three sons, she lives in the "Citrus Capital of the World"—Santa Paula, California, with her husband, Larry, and youngest son, Chris. They are members of the Ventura Missionary Church. Kathi spends her time reading, walking, doing aerobics, going camping with her family, and writing "anything and everything" on her computer.

213